DIVINE WISDOM

Messages of Love, Hope and Healing from the Masters

LISA WILLIAMS

Animal Dreaming Publishing
www.AnimalDreamingPublishing.com

Divine Wisdom
Messages of Love, Hope and Healing from the Masters

ANIMAL DREAMING PUBLISHING
PO Box 5203 East Lismore NSW 2480
AUSTRALIA
Phone +61 2 6622 6147
www.AnimalDreamingPublishing.com
www.facebook.com/AnimalDreamingPublishing
Email: publish@animaldreamingpublishing.com

First published 2018
Copyright text © 2018 Lisa Williams

Cover Copyright © Animal Dreaming Pubishing
Design and Layout Copyright © Animal Dreaming Publishing

ISBN: 978-0-648245575

The information in this book is intended for spiritual and emotional guidance only. It is not intended to replace medical advice or treatment.

Designed by Animal Dreaming Publishing
Printed in Australia

For all my students, clients and fans who have supported me throughout the years; You gave me the confidence to find the real source of knowledge and to realize that having a gift that is pure is something worth following. Thank you for your love and support.

To Colleen
Sending love &
Blessings
luv xx

CONTENTS

INTRODUCTION

I received a channeled message (below) years ago when I was writing a course on advanced mediumship. It wasn't the first message I had received in my life but this particular one was special for me. It was overwhelming and powerful. Many teachers say, 'Always keep a notebook by your bed,' but a laptop was the only thing that I could grab as this channeled wisdom was being downloaded into my consciousness.

It was a gloomy night and the mood was gloomy too. At 3am I was in a hotel room with my son Charlie, who was peacefully sleeping in the next bed, when I suddenly sat upright and started tapping away at the keyboard. My fingers flew across the screen as if they were not attached to my body, and the information flowed through my body and onto the page. It was only when I sat back and started to read did I realize what I had written.

It was very reflective of my personal journey but it was specifically for my students who I was about to start teaching. It was also for others who were already on their journey with Spirit, as it demonstrated that Spirit will always be there for them in this ever-changing world.

My message from the Masters

When you work with us, you are working with yourself. You are working for your highest good and also for the grace of God and Spirit.

Sadly, everyone's world has become consumed by life.

This is a special time in your existence. Minds are coming together for a reason: to spread the messages in a world that has forgotten what is real and needs so much healing. Those that are among you are opening up to the world that we live in – which is the world that you have come from – and are educating those who have forgotten their way.

We will serve you well if you serve us. Many extraordinary things may happen to you while you're working with and for us. That is because we will reward you for your service.

Open your eyes and start to live your life with the realization that your destiny is within the very contains of you and that you're on the right pathway.

Yes, your life may have been tough and difficult but that was for a reason. You have been guided to take this road of hardship so that you can journey with other souls and help them through life. Do you think that we enjoy watching you suffer without us? No, we don't but we will always guide you well and help you take each step through your journey.

Some steps may be harder than others but through this work, you will find the courage to open your eyes and learn that you are fulfilling your destiny and dreams.

Know that you are loved always and no one is going to judge you. Those who judge you do not understand you, nor do they understand life and do not live life to its fullest. You cannot change those people but they are put in your pathway to test you and you can survive those tests. And you will always come out smiling.

You won't win as it's not a game and if you think about it that way, your ego will come alive again and this is something that you can ill afford. You have to rise above them and enjoy the challenge.

May your heart always be open, keep a smile on your face and your arms outstretched for the embrace that is so needed by others to heal.

We wish you well on your journey through Spirit.

* * *

I became a trance channel purely by accident. One Saturday afternoon I was sitting in a stranger's bedroom giving private readings to a group of women in Handsworth Wood, Birmingham. I was in my 20s and had been out late the night before and so I blamed my tiredness on that, but was nevertheless holding the energy for Spirit. I sat there in front of a client who was Indian and started her reading. I felt like I needed to close my eyes, so I did. I was still talking and I could hear myself in my head but soon I found myself slipping away and my voice was in the distance.

With a gasp I opened my eyes and I looked at this poor woman who was sitting there with her mouth wide open. I apologized for falling asleep for a second but she asked me to stop talking while she grabbed out of my hand the tape player that was recording the session. She rewound it and urgently said, 'Listen.'

Through the crackles and hissing of the tape I could hear a man speaking a different language to her. It was her father who had channeled through me speaking Punjabi. You can imagine my shock as she ran downstairs to her friends and made them all listen to the recording. Even though I was drained after that experience, it was incredible to think that a spirit could overtake my body. I had only seen it in the movie *Ghost*, and even then I was skeptical. But that was the first of countless times that Spirit has channeled through me and given me inspirational messages.

Natural law, life, lessons, guidance and love are all topics that Spirit talks about and I have found throughout my time as a trance channel, the questions that have been asked of the 'Masters' are all based around these. I have been compelled to share these channeled messages for years, but it was only recently that I was informed that I didn't have a choice; I had been chosen by Spirit to be the scribe for the Elders. If I had received this message from my own Spirits, I would have questioned whether it was my mind overthinking the message and allowing my own Lisa ego to step forward, but this time it was different.

I was in Australia when I went to visit Maria Eilta, a well-known healer who had a crystal bed. Yes, a crystal bed, and my mind was thinking it could be all woo woo; however, I had laid on her bed a few years before and I didn't remember much about the experience except that it was really relaxing.

I turned up at her apartment on one of my only days off and we sat on her balcony overlooking the Gold Coast. I was mesmerized by the waves as they crashed on the shore of the beautiful ocean that lay before me. After enjoying that moment of sitting with a like-minded soul and talking about the universe and life, Maria got up and started to prepare this huge bed that looked like something from a sci-fi movie and told me to get on top of it. It was as if she had been guided at that exact moment to start the healing.

I'm not one to argue, especially when someone has a gift. I'm open to any experience that life has to offer, so climbing on, I was careful not to bang my head on the pyramid that had been created over the platform of the bed. I lay down, and immediately felt a buzzing; I actually thought the bed was plugged into the electric power point, which was my human skeptical mind wavering for a moment but this soon dissipated when I noticed she was strategically placing crystals around me. The buzzing and vibration became more intense and before I knew it, I felt I felt like I was spinning around from the energy. Simply amazing!

I didn't think much more about it and lay there listening to the ocean crashing on the shore, feeling the breeze coming in through the open patio door and remaining connected to the energy. I was in heaven. Blissfully happy to bask in the natural energy of crystals that were around me.

When the session ended, she sat me down and she started to tell me all the things that had been 'downloaded' to her during my time on the bed. Over the years I have had many different readings but I didn't expect this one to reduce me to tears and leave me sitting contemplating the next stages of my life. I have always been a medium and it's something that I had thought I would always do, but when I heard her words, I sat there not knowing what to say.

You are to be the scribe for the Elders.
It's non-negotiable, Lisa.
We are calling you the Master and it's your job to be their voice.

And this experience finally confirmed my feelings that the channeled messages I had been receiving shouldn't be kept to myself – that they should be shared around the world to give hope, inspiration and peace to those who need it.

The Masters, as I refer to them, are a team. I don't know exactly who gives what message but I know it's a higher force of energy. A collective group of souls that are not Guides but are the Divine light of love. They have been referred to as the Elders, the Council of Elders, Spirit and the Divine, but to me they are simply the Masters.

I am aware of some of the Masters and call them my team, such as Ben (my Master Guide), and Anu, Josiah and Ariel (Elders). But sometimes it's a divine connection of energy that surges through me like a lightning bolt and the energy is very different, sacred and pure. It's these messages that I have been guided to share with you.

HOW TO USE
THIS BOOK

L ife continually presents us with the need for answers, which is why people seek out psychics and mediums. But often this desire for guidance is immediate and getting through the day can be overwhelming, especially when experiencing loss and where healing is needed. And it's then that I tell people to take it 'moment by moment'.

Sitting alone with our thoughts can send us into a spiral of despair, particularly if we don't know where or how to find peace. In our search for hope we then overthink. We do our best to connect to Spirit but our intuition falters and we can become lost. Every single person on this Earth has had a moment like that and has not known what to do, myself included.

It's during this time that we need to stop, breathe and re-center. 'Easier said than done,' I hear you say! But by simply taking a minute to focus and do the following will help you center yourself.:

- Count your breaths in and out of your body.
- Then open this book to a page that you are guided to and read the passage.
- Allow it to sink in.
- Then read it again.

It is here, in the Masters' messages, that you will find the answers you need.

There are many ways that *Divine Wisdom* can help you. You may wish to read a passage daily and let that be your daily inspiration or you may wish to read the book in its entirety. Whichever you decide, it is the right way for you. Even though there are sections that are dedicated to different topics, there is a message for everyone, no matter which passage you read.

Trust your intuition and allow the knowledge to penetrate into your soul.

Enjoy!

The wonders of the Spirit World

The wonders of the Spirit World will never cease to amaze you but it's when they do that you must stop. Stop and get back to the wonder of being a child again with your eyes open wide to the world in amazement and fascination.

We will prepare you for your journey of enlightening souls and sharing in the gift that we call our own: the gift of Spirit.

We are Spirit.

You are Spirit.

The world is Spirit.

The universal light that shines on in the world.

The gift of hope, of compassion, of understanding, of love but most all, of healing.

You will heal souls as you walk along the pathway and open hearts and minds to the world beyond.

You are not teachers, you are a creation of the loving energy that you call God.

You are the creation of the sole purpose for mankind, which is to heal.

Nothing and no one can to do this single-handedly, so you have been chosen to guide the way - the way forward that no one else knows.

You are on this journey for a reason. You have been guided for a reason - to help others grow and to see the light. The light that in many people burns so low. You will stimulate that flame and you will change the lives of many you meet, one by one, creating a ripple effect throughout the world. A world that needs changing and needs healing.

You are not alone. The Masters walk with you every step of the way. When the journey becomes too much, we will take you back to the truth with integrity. A truth so far beyond what you know already.

Step into the pathway of power and change and know that you can open the hearts of those you meet. Guide those who walk with you as you lead others through the loving embrace of Spirit. As you lead them on journey that may feel isolated but is enriched with love. A love that lasts an eternity and grows intensely, daily.

We can only do so much but as long as your heart and mind is open to receive, we can move through you like a dance of two lovers entwined in the romance of music.

Honor this journey and allow the rest to follow. You will change for all to see and those who do not want that change in you, will move aside to enable the love of Spirit to rise. Those who see this within you, will stand with you and watch you blossom with pride and love.

Honor your word, your love and your soul.

Bring forward the light that you have been given and touch others in a way that you have been touched.

You are the change in the world that we need. Light the way forward for others to follow.

It's a new day, a new beginning and a time in which to embrace all that you are.

You are the messenger of light and we entrust you with our knowledge and love.

Chapter 1

SURRENDERING

Referring to the Divine has been somewhat new to me over the last few years, yet it's a phrase you will hear me saying more and more. I never believed in God but I wanted to be a nun – how ironic! What is interesting though, even as a young child I had a calling. A calling greater than anything I could have ever imagined. In my innocent and naive days, I didn't know how that looked so the only way I could quantify it was in the desire to be a nun. And I wasn't even Catholic!

It really was my mother and grandmother that set me on this pathway. I certainly never expected the outcome, especially having an atheist as a father. But Wednesday nights were mother and daughter nights and we would go to the local spiritual church to watch the medium deliver messages. I'll be honest, the only reason we were going was to watch the mediums demonstrate their gifts while we hoped and prayed to get some 'message' from our loved ones that we were on the right track. Naturally, we prayed to the 'God' that they were talking about and hoped that Spirit would come through, but the more I attended, the more I started to see the truth and the power that Spirit had given me.

It was much earlier in life that I had a 'spiritual awakening'. It was summer and I was about 14 years old. Diamond Farm was the home of our caravan where I spent the summers. I knew everyone and would see the same people visiting every year. We made friends forever. At the time, I was one of those irritable, annoying, Miss-Goody-Two-Shoes who was into everything, including welcoming the newcomers of Diamond Farm to the park and making sure that everyone had a good time. The Sunshine Club was a religious organization that brought children away for a few weeks to have fun, but to also embrace the word of God; of course, I was part of their welcoming committee and had to get involved!

I wasn't quite fully believing in God at the time due to my atheist family, even though I wanted to be a nun, but I did question 'What if?'. That was always my motto because of my grandfather who always said, 'Never get to my age and think, "What if?" Get to my age and say, "I've had a bloody good time and I don't regret a thing"'. So that's what I did.

One night I found myself agreeing to go with the Sunshine Club to their church meeting in the local village hall, which is where I used to go on the weekends when Nan wanted to play bingo. I never considered it to be a religious place of worship, but sitting there I remember being taken in by their service. Of course, they were talking about the Bible and the biblical stories that were written many centuries after the fact, but it was more than that. It was a belief and something to have faith in. It was a truth that some live their lives by. It was the guidance that many needed to get through difficulties. It was the written word of truth and love.

We bowed our heads in prayer and the minister asked if there was anyone who wanted to surrender their life to God and to serve him. My mind was almost laughing as I thought, 'Who is going to serve a fictitious figure that we have given this power to and who isn't even real or alive?' But I found my hand raised above my head, and although I was trying to forcefully yank it down, it stayed high in the air. Dread and fear took over as someone guided me to the front where the minister waited and he then asked me to surrender myself to Jesus and God.

This couldn't be happening. The 14-year-old self was glad that none of her school friends were watching, because although religion was a big part of the Church of England school I went to, no one really paid attention.

It's ironic thinking back to that awkward night of surrendering to God, as it's now something that I do daily. It was in that uncomfortable moment that I found comfort. I said my first ever prayer aloud. I mean I had said prayers before, but they were more along the lines of: 'Oh God, please don't let my parents find out about...' But this time I was asking God to forgive me for my wrongdoings and to grace me with his presence as I continued to walk in life. As I muttered the words 'Amen', I suddenly felt WHOLE. Weird, really. It was as if I was experiencing an understanding, a knowing and a belief. A belief that I could be what God wanted me to be. I still think back to that day as my kind of awakening.

Yet, I struggled with the word God – the one power that unites us together – because it didn't feel like it was merely one soul, to me it felt more than that. And so, my search commenced, and continued. While religion can divide many people who hold the same beliefs, the terminology itself can confuse, segregate and divide us to the point of hatred. It certainly didn't align with my feelings, thoughts and newfound beliefs. I struggled with it for many years until I found myself surrendering to my roots, where my grandmother had found her peace; the religion of spiritualism where I was finally home.

Walking into the Church of the Living Spirit (it had been fondly nicknamed the happy church) and hearing them say, 'We are an independent spiritualist church that supports the God of your own understanding. We practice, promote and teach unconditional love', was music to my ears! Everyone joined together to recite the principles:

- We believe in God.
- We believe that God is all there is.

- We affirm the divine right of individuals to seek the truth within their own hearts.

- Life is eternal.

- Spiritual progression is eternal and infinite.

- We believe that communication between all planes of existence is a reality.

- The ultimate expression of loving God is to love thy neighbor as thyself.

- We believe in personal responsibility and each individual creates their own reality according to natural law.

- We affirm the innate gifts of mediumship and healing are expressions of God's love.

Wow... This represented everything I believed in and meant I could honor the God of my own understanding, which I called the 'Divine'. To this day, for me it is a word that encompasses everything without limitations.

Surrendering to the Divine has become my life, my word and my work. The Divine light shines within us all and it's time to trust and surrender to the grace and beauty that opens the doorway to the knowledge that we need.

With these messages from the Masters, all you have to do is listen and be guided through life.

Surrender to the Divine

The journey is about awakening - awakening your soul to discover the beauty that you seek, and which is within you. It's a guiding force that is the one solitary promise that we can give you.

You are the love and love will surround you in all that you do. This is the power of the soul. Divine guidance will lead you to the powerful source of growth and love.

You are the power.

You are the source.

You are the Divine.

The Divine is within you and the journey that you seek is golden. The ray of light will flow from your very being and touch others on this path.

Open your heart to the wealth of tomorrow. Open your mind to the journey ahead of you.

The transitional time that you need is right before you. It's there within reach. Reach out and touch it.

Believe in this moment.

You are the change others will seek.

You are the knowledge that others will pursue.

You are the one that loves from the soul.

Your destiny is set.

You speak of truth.

You search beyond the soul's purpose. Never faltering or floundering and you will shine.

Let go of beliefs, structure and control. You will have the power to surrender. Surrender to the Divine Wisdom that you carry in your soul by capturing your Divine and bringing forth the wisdom and knowledge of your journey.

Be free, be joyous and enjoy, for you are a messenger of the light.

The sea of change

The power that is beneath you is immense and immeasurable, yet you must surrender to the guidance and the love of Spirit and God, to the peace and love that we all possess. When you surrender, you release the control of the ego and that of the mind.

The ego, which is the true force that holds you in a cycle in life.

It's in the release of this cycle and the not knowing that gives you the power to be in the place that you need to be in. The surrounding force of the Divine will set you forth on the pathway of purpose. We will lead you to the place of forgiveness and of truth, and will show you the light that is needed to survive the ever-changing world in which you live. It's the blinding light that shines when you can't see the path. Trust it, for it's the path that you need to walk on and it's the path that will lead you to the truth.

When you don't know your way forward, you will surrender to the place of not knowing. Because, when you can see the journey ahead, your human inclination is to control every bump and obstacle along the way.

But what is the beauty in that? What is the lesson and what will you learn?

Nothing, my friend, as you need to let go of control and be in the space of being. Being the true source of the light is what you will need to give others guidance along the way.

When you lead, others will follow. It's the natural law of life, the ripple effect in the sea of change.

You are the change that others need to see.

Don't fear this, or it will take control. Simply live and let go. Let go of all control and when you can truly master the release, you will see the opportunities that present themselves. The opportunities that you never saw being fulfilled at the beginning of change.

Let go, trust and believe. Open your heart and mind, and believe in all that you are and allow the Divine to do the rest. If the pathway is to be, it will be.

The Divine light will guide you home.

Healing channeling

Healing, ah, what a beautiful gift it is to heal, to close the wound, to take away the hurt, pain and the suffering that holds you back. How to heal is a somewhat unknown and not everyone knows how it will happen. Not everyone does it the same as another. No one healing moment is the same as another.

It's the thought and the mind that holds you back in the knowledge of keeping that pain alive; the pain of the hurt.

Healing is acceptance. Healing is love, and healing is honoring what has happened, to open the wound and then to release the pain that holds you, locks you into place and makes you captive.

Let go of the pain and start to accept. Acceptance is the key that brings about love that brings about knowledge that brings about wisdom. It is the understanding of where you have come from that can lead you forward into the future to heal.

The healing can be a moment, it can be a day, it can be a week, or it can be a lifetime. Some people are on a journey of healing wounds that have affected lives before, previous moments that they have carried forward into the energy of this life. This life is where they can renew their soul; where they can renew their body and renew the knowledge that they have to let go of the past and to start again like a butterfly that goes through the transformation of change.

The wisdom that is shared with so many enlightens the day. That one touch, that one smile, that one look, just a nod can change the lives of many and start the healing anew.

It is time now to step forward with the acceptance that it is time to heal. Time to let go of the restriction of pain and to step into the peaceful side of that space of love. Love is what encompasses everything. It comes from within the heart space where you can wrap yourself up into that place of love.

The healing is there; the healing is one. Acceptance is the key.

Time to move forward. Open your heart. Surround yourself with the vibration of love from the love of Spirit and God.

Your soul beauty

The soul beauty is yours to take. It's the understanding of truth that comes from within that enables your soul to soar into the vast open space. The space that is called infinity.

Infinity is so vast, you may not be able to comprehend it. It's in this place that love can grow. It's in this place that wounds can heal. It's in this place where love flows and the truth lays within your heart, not your mind. Let your mind be free of the captivity that you create. You create this captivity within the restraints of what you want your life to be.

Open your mind, let go and live in the truth of the soul. The soul which is beauty, the soul which is truth.

No one can understand and comprehend the space in which you live. You live in a vast world of togetherness, yet you live as one. One in a world that needs to unite as a front to move forward and together create the beauty of mankind. Open the heart and space for it's yours to see. This is beyond the knowledge that your human mind will understand. This is beyond the knowledge of comprehension. Yet trust. Trust in what you know. The beauty is there, in the vast space that you live.

Get down deep into the soul, into that place that is home. A place of home, a place of truth and a place of beauty. Just trust and we will always be on the journey with you.

See what we see.

Feel the truth.

Feel the emotion.

Allow yourself to emerge into the beauty beyond.

Trust and believe in all that you have.

Open your eyes, dig deep down inside into the soul, release the restrictions on your mind and there you will find truth.

The restricting mind

So, you want to talk about the restrictions of the mind. It's simple: you think, you restrict. You don't think, you're open. The ego comes alive. The ego is only your thoughts that are projected out into the universe and as you know, those projected thoughts become alive within your own understanding of life.

The truth of the matter is that there is no one or thing that is controlling you, except you. No spirit, no one and no self.

The restrictions that you put upon yourself - the things you say you cannot do - are all within the mind.

When you let go of the thought patterns that are producing these restrictions, the world can be endless. Endless and beyond what you can ever know. The beauty is waiting there to captivate you and seeing past the darkness will unearth this beauty. Let go of the restrictions and the light will shine upon you.

All you have to do is look. Take away the ego, take away the mind, take away the thoughts and be. Sit in a place of rest, understand that this is your time - nothing more, nothing less, nothing to take - and just be still.

Understand that this is your gift, the gift of the universe that is given to you. Breathe. Every breath that you take is the new breath of a new life, the new life that you are about to embark on. Each breath holds so much, it is the light that comes in and releases. The breath is the start of the journey forward. Not a step but a breath.

The breath is courage. The breath is confidence. The breath is strength. Take the breath and believe in what it can hold for you.

Let go of the restrictions of the mind, take that breath and move forward.

Chapter 2

SPIRITUALITY

I grew up in a small town in England and was given an opportunity to come to America. Nothing or no one prepared me for the journey that lay ahead. It was a gift that was literally handed to me whether I wanted it or not and in a flash, my life changed.

I was driving over the canyon towards the television studio in North Hollywood where I was recording my show *Life Among the Dead* when Dallas, who worked for Merv Griffin, asked me, 'What are you going to do when you finish filming the show?'

My response was simple. 'I'm going to go back to doing my readings daily.'

He laughed and I was completely confused by his reaction.

'Lisa, your life will never be the same again after this.' And he was right. My life changed in the blink of an eye.

I completely surrendered to the life that had been handed to me by some amazing people who I worked with. I felt blessed and am thankful for the way it has turned out. Even to my ex-husband who initiated the trip to America in the first place, because I wouldn't be where I am right now. Content and happy.

For eight years, life in Los Angeles was fun, exciting and my feet hardly touched the ground. I was a single working mom with an extraordinary life: working hard, doing readings and at the same time pursuing my dreams of traveling, teaching and speaking globally, all while raising my son. It may sound amazing and glamorous but it wasn't easy. I sacrificed many things to bring my work to the masses and to help healing on a larger scale. It was something that I knew I had to do... it was my calling.

But the sacrifices were to the detriment of my son. In his younger years he traveled the world and lived a life by my side, but reality had to happen, I had to be the responsible parent and keep him in school and so I found myself traveling without him and losing out on some valuable years of his life. He never complained or was sad it was our life.

My parents would come over from Spain (where they live) and help, along with friends, and I was blessed and thankful to have people in my life who loved my son as their own, because I couldn't have done it without them.

It was on one of those many voyages that my life changed. I didn't know it at the time and I actually resisted it for a long time. Again, here is the human element of control that we all possess.

I had been asked by many people to go to this place called Lily Dale. I had never heard of it and my Los Angeles ego was thinking, 'I haven't heard of it, so it's not something I should do'. Looking back, I realize I had been consumed by ego. The realization of that is hard enough but to experience what happened next is worse.

I woke up one morning examining my life and suddenly thought, 'Lisa, I don't like you'. Quite an eye-opening experience for your own self to see who you are. It was then that I stopped resisting and surrendered to who I wanted to be.

Yes, I was a medium, but that didn't mean *I* had to be spiritual and I could still connect without having to do anything further. But I had been bitten by the lifestyle that had been created and it was time to stop, time to be who I truly was.

A few weeks later I was at an authors' dinner at a Hay House for *I Can do It* when Sandra Anne Taylor and Sharon Klinger invited me to go to Lily Dale. Again, there it was, that place.

'You would love it,' they said. 'You will be the season's highlight'.

I had no idea what they were talking about. But I agreed and that was that. Little did I know that this was the start of a new chapter in my life.

Waking up on a bright July morning in a room that was a throwback to the 1800s, the only sign that indicated I was in the modern day was the hum of the air conditioner. Yes, I was in Lily Dale, but I still didn't know much about the place. I could hear people chatting underneath my window as they were heading to the coffee shop and cars driving past the Assembly Hall. I had arrived in the dark so I couldn't see much but now, as I looked out of my window, I realized my room was overlooking a beautiful lake and park with people meditating, laughing and being excited about the day ahead.

I was in a daze and had no concept of the enormity of this small village near Buffalo NY.

The one thing that stuck in my mind from that first visit was driving down a pebbled forest-lined pathway in a golf cart with Sharon Klinger. She was excited to show me this trail and a 'stump'. I was so confused! We started to slow down and the trees broke to reveal hundreds of people sitting on benches and standing at the back. I heard a booming voice coming from a short red-headed woman, 'Good Afternoon!' I realize now that it was Jessie Furst, one of Lily Dale's registered mediums.

I sat down underneath the trees and watched medium after medium go up to what looked like a large tree stump and deliver messages. I was completely in awe and thought, 'Wow, they have places like this in the world dedicated to mediumship and Spirit!' I was in heaven.

Sharon asked me, 'Do you want to go up and deliver some messages?' I found myself nodding and thinking, 'What are you doing, Lisa? Are you mad?'

I sat there nervously, my stomach in knots, in my left brain and head, thinking, 'What if you can't do this? What if you don't do it right?'. It was completely out of character for me, as I was on stage night after night and delivered messages to thousands around the world, and here I was nervous about standing in front of a tree stump to give three messages.

As my name was called I was referred to as a 'visiting medium from LA' and I could hear the whispers of people as they turned and nudged their friends. All eyes were on me. If only they knew how nervous I was. Those three messages were the quickest messages I had ever delivered and I can't even remember them. But what I do remember was standing there and feeling the energy of the ground around me, the tress rustling in the slight breeze on that hot afternoon, the overwhelming connection to Spirit, and that it was like falling into a loving embrace of Spirit. They supported me and I felt peace. I was home!

The whole trip was a whirlwind and for days after I wondered where I had been. That's when I started to research it: Lily Dale Assembly, The World's Largest Center for the Religion of Spiritualism. I couldn't believe that there was a little village in the middle of nowhere that dedicated itself to mediumship, the continuity of life and spiritualism; a religion that I had been involved in for years. Why hadn't I known about this sanctuary before?

It became a yearly trip, each time extending the amount of time I had there. I would wander around the beautiful grounds of the village set in a lush forest. It was an escape from the rat race that LA had become for me. I'd drive through the gates and be thrown back to the 1800s where people had a smile on their faces and were friendly. And where I was greeted like I was a friend.

'Hey, Lisa Williams. Come and ride in my Model T,' a voice said out of nowhere, and suddenly I was being embraced with a big hug by a man who now happens to be my neighbor and friend, Greg Ford. Before I knew it, I was in this old Model T and being driven around the grounds. I had so much fun and was in a place that I looked forward to visiting yearly, but I wanted to stay somewhere else on the grounds, I wasn't sure where but I wanted to be somewhere different.

My assistant Karen started the hunt, and in her search she discovered a place that I could stay. I had decided to stay for a week this time, which was the longest time I had every stayed, and Natalie Larson opened her home to me. Sitting there on the porch, watching people wander around the grounds was peaceful and relaxing. I visited the 'Inspiration Stump' where I had delivered my first message a few years before and realized that it was a perfect place of reflection and contemplation. The museum was insightful and Ron Nagy gave me a potted history of the Fox Sisters and their spirit rappings in 1848 that started modern-day mediumship. The forest temple was the highlight of my afternoon; a gentle loving energy of spirit connections and then the healing temple... Wow! The energy and healing that flowed through the building and surrounding areas was like riding a cloud of love. I spent my days walking, reading and writing.

Being a nosy person, I wanted to take a peek into one of the homes for sale that was a few doors down, never expecting what happened next. I walked through the double doors and I heard the house, or Spirit, say to me, 'Welcome home'. I was floored. I walked into this impeccable house, fell in love and never wanted to leave.

Less than six months later, Charlie and I spent our first white Christmas in our new Lily Dale home surrounded by people who we didn't know but who embraced us with love. It was unbelievable, and six months after that we started a road trip to drive across America to spend the whole summer in Lily Dale; it was certainly a memorable trip for various reasons.

Charlie had found his voice. He hated Lily Dale. It was too quiet and there was nothing to do. What was he going to do in LA? Play video games all summer?

I was forcing him to get out into nature and to be present. As a child in today's society, going outside to play was somewhat alien. When I told him he could go anywhere he wanted as long as he didn't go out of the gates, he couldn't understand that I had given him freedom without worrying. He certainly wasn't going to get lost and I knew he was a good kid so he wouldn't get into trouble, but one day he returned angry after sitting in the woods for a few hours.

How can anyone get angry hunting for sticks in the woods? As awful as it was, something remarkable had happened. His energy had shifted and circumstances that he had held locked so deep within him had surfaced and hit him in the face. I had never seen him so angry but I was thankful for that day.

'I hate my life, I hate your work, I hate your travel. I don't want a celebrity, I want a mom,' he yelled, slammed the door and ran up two flights of steep stairs to his room. Bewildered, I sat on the kitchen floor sobbing. At the time I didn't like what I was hearing but reality had hit me between the eyes. He was right. He needed his mom and not someone who only came home to do laundry and to change the suitcase. I heard heavy footsteps on the stairs and he ran out of the house. I knew he needed space but we also needed to talk. Two hours went by and it was getting dark. I started to panic about where he was and then I found him, back in the woods sitting on a felled tree. We then talked for the first time in a long time. We truly connected and I made a pact to him that I would slow down and he would be my priority until he had a life of his own.

I honestly believe that something in Lily Dale's energy, the home of free thinkers, mediums and new thought, gave him a voice and he found the strength to open himself up and heal. People always went to Charlie for healing but this time Charlie came here to start his healing journey. It was then I knew I had to leave LA.

Spirit provides for us in ways that you can never imagine, and it was less than four months later that I was leaving Los Angeles. Lily Dale is a place that changed my life and world forever. As my life took shape over the past 10 years, while dedicating my world to Spirit I had found home in a place that dedicates itself to spiritualism and Spirit. It was the perfect combination.

My life has since slowed down but it was through surrendering to Spirit that it's taken a new course in the way that I work. Again, the ever-flowing energy of the Divine that will change the course of life as it's needed.

I find solace at the stump throughout the year, and the writings that come from the collective of Spirit are enlightening and inspiring. Here is the first of many that were written at Inspiration Stump.

A message from the stump

All you need to do is believe in the power of thought, the power of prayer and believe in yourself.

Spirit will guide and you will follow.

The surrounding negativity will show you the light and highlight the dark. It will show you what you need and what you do not want.

It will share with you the wonders of the world and help you see the pathway forward and the way that you need to grow. It's time to believe in the power of YOU, no one else but you. It's time to believe all that you can be and all that you are. No one is going to change that. It's time that you realized the diversity of the truth, the diversity of the power and the power that you have.

You are among the gifted few and the one that we have chosen to step into the space of change. You are the one that will change this space.

Own your power and believe in your journey. You are the one force that needs to shine and when others darken your way, your light will shine brighter. Yes, you will learn and you will see your truth but you will see the truth within your own heart and you will come back to the space of being and the power that was always there.

We chose you to illuminate the way forward. You are the pioneer and the glory that is needed for this. We have answered your prayers and we are seeing you through. Just trust in all that you have.

Know that your journey is just beginning and that the light of the way is shining for you.

Follow your heart and your dreams and know that it is in the very essence of this that you will rise above it all and shine through.

We are working with you, my friend, and believe in all that you have and all that you know. We are proud of you and we stand in truth along your way.

Your dreams are shining for all to see and it's time to follow your light to the pathway of tomorrow and to believe in your heart that you can follow that light and find your dream; it's in the very space that you can find home. Home: your soul. Your being. Your everything. You are everything that is needed for life – you create the journey and you are the life force for you.

Breathe and allow the acceptance in your heart to move forward with your dreams and your life. No one will change that. Some will try but with the force so strong, you will journey into that world of trust and know that you will be guided by Spirit. Spirit, the everlasting loyal friend of yours, is everywhere. Trust in the guidance that you are seeing and being given.

Allow the ego to fade into the distance and know that you will be journeying forward in the way that is right for you. You are on the very pathway that you have chosen; every step, every thought and every whisper is there for you to see. It's around you, flourishing and growing – just believe in all that you have and all that you are.

Follow your dreams and know that you are the only one that has the control to change this, no one else. And no one can unless you submit your power to those around you. We love you and have faith in the strength in the love that you have.

It's time to take the first step, my friend, on the journey that will lead to the dream.

Seize the moment

Opening the pathway beyond to what you can be is sometimes unimaginable, and it's only when you experience the unimaginable that it becomes imaginable.

You have the opportunity to live in the way that you need to live and only you have the right to say what the pathway is for you on this journey through life.

Open your mind to the expanse of the universe and see the answers that are given you for all will unfold in the way that you need it to. Today is only the beginning of your journey. It's the beginning right now and you will have the space and the time to create and recreate all that you need in life.

You are the very beginning of your soul. Tomorrow will be another beginning and when you see life this way, you will see the opportunities that are presented.

Never close a door that is still wide open. It's there for a reason, but if you feel it's time to walk away then you must trust in your heart with what you need to do. We will be with you every step of the way.

The beginning will resurface again for you so that you can see the sun shining and hear the music in your ears as you dance through the journey of life. Because you have been given the opportunities right now.

Seize the moment and take all that is given to you. Never fear, your love for Spirit will guide you on this pathway.

We believe in you!

We are all one

We are all one. You are one with us and we are one with you. The universe is a place where you are able to connect to each other through souls. The connection you need with us is available through a feeling, a thought or a whisper. Just a moment in your lifetime and your world.

Opening your heart to the love that is beyond is all that you need to do to connect. We are with you, now and always.

Throughout your life you only have to connect to us and ask us to be with you. We will show you that we are here.

The love that we have is immeasurable.

Your evolution throughout life has bought you to this point. The point where, only now, this moment is guaranteed and tomorrow is a blessing.

Open your eyes to the mysteries and wonders of where life is taking you. Rid yourself of control and fear and journey with us, allowing us to guide you.

Listen with your heart and mind and know that we love you and you will be supported in all that you do.

Surrender and give thanks to what you have before you right now.

We love you and will be always watching over you.

The ripple effect

Taking the power that you have been given is fulfilling, enlightening and courageous. It takes courage for you to stand on your own, to make your own decisions and to believe in yourself. Not everyone can do this and when you stand alone and stand up, you are the power of change.

One person standing up for change encourages others to also and united, the ripple effect takes place and you stand together for the greater good of all.

Goodness in your heart is all that you need to start the circle of spiritual growth.

Believing that there can be a change and there will be a change: this is something that takes strength. Your strength will shine through giving others the courage to find their own strength to get through another day. This strength grows over a period of time and slowly, life becomes easier and that smile on your face is no longer forced - it's a true smile of happiness.

That happiness is infectious and when you smile others smile too, which in turn creates the smile of happiness around you, the circle of courage and the chain of strength; all of which society is crying out for. It's a movement of hope. It's the way forward in life. It's the understanding that tomorrow can be a brighter future and knowing that whatever comes your way is intentional so that you can help yourself and others to grow.

This is a time of change and one where courage, hope, strength and happiness is needed.

We are proud of the work that you are doing and it's time that others followed your example.

Be well, my friend, and know that you are the change that the world needs.

You are everything that you need

Opening your heart to the wonders of the day is always a joy. Standing strong and believing in who you are is all that you need for seeing the future that will manifest in front of you.

Stand in your power and be truthful to your life, your love and yourself. You are the love that you seek, you are the joy that you yearn for, and you are the hope that you need. You are everything that you need.

Just allow your light to shine through and believe and surrender into the moment of now.

That is all you need right now; nothing more or nothing less. It's time to own your life and who you are. You are courageous, loving, kind and caring and you know authenticity.

Never waver because you will be guided on this pathway with hope and comfort, trust and love. Your journey will start with Spirit and end with Spirit. All you need to do is see what we see in you and trust, breathe and enjoy the journey with Spirit by your side.

You are truly loved, my friend.

Times of change

As times change and tomorrows become yesterdays, look at the world in wonder like you did as a child.

You are the hope and the natural beauty that excels in the world.

You have the power to make the change that is being sought.

You are the voice that others will listen to.

You have the honor and the will to succeed in life.

You are everything because the world begins with you.

You are the driving force that others will seek.

You are the openness for the air that you breathe.

You are the Divine force that is being led for others to follow.

Believe in all that you are and all of this will be.

You are the true beauty that shines in the world of endless possibilities and hope.

The Masters that walk among you will open the doors for you.

The guidance that you need will be given.

You are the light in the world and the light will shine bright before you to follow, all you have to do is believe. Cherish the moments as you move forward, leaving the past behind and joining the world before you.

And this world will become a better place because your tomorrow will be joyous and full of love. Give all you wish to receive and allow the light to shine through.

Speak the truth

Stay strong and be in your power and do not waver on all that you want. Standing your ground will give you all that you want and need. What your ego wants is worthless, as your soul is not speaking.

Your soul will say something else and you can stand in your power when you speak from this place. Your ego's expectations leave you feeling hollow and empty, but your soul knows the truth and allows the truth to flow through you like a river flowing through the body of land on the place that you call Earth.

Remember that you are here to fulfill your contract with the people that are both in your life and those who are yet to come.

You are on a pathway of change and to accept this change as part of the learning - grown and molded like glass that is being blown together. This bond is delicate, yet strong.

When your souls know one another, the rest will follow. Allow the ego to fade into the distance and be the one that others want to be like.

You are a leader of your own destiny and you are, therefore, the powerful source of your own horizon.

Speak from the heart and speak the truth. Seek your answers from your soul.

Believe that you are in the right place at the right time and know that your faith will carry you through.

Bring peace into your world and grow!

I love you, my friend.

Divine goddess

During one of my many visits to Inspiration Stump, I sat not knowing what to ask for but allowed Spirit to give me what I needed. I was discovering myself on a new level; something totally different to what I had experienced before. I suddenly felt a goddess energy rising through me and my pen started to write with a flowing energy.

This message is powerful and helps me see the light when I have self-doubt. Enjoy!

You are on a journey and an everlasting one. You have the power to support your own dreams and your values will remain high for all to see.

You now have choice in life and this journey that you are on is extended to the highest heights. You are worthy of so much and you need to dream big bigger than you have ever done.

You will be given so much and it's time because you have started to re-evaluate and cut the loose ends and express what you need. It's time to only do what you need and this is why I am here.

You are the goddess of power and all that you create will be applied and allowed for only a few to see.

I am here to help you step into the goddess power that you embody and to help you believe in your dreams. You have been the warrior for many others but now it's time to open your space and expand beyond. Your limits have been freed and you are the universe of power and the eternal force and light that others seek.

You are the goddess of one. The phoenix will rise like never before and you will own your world and the universe will be yours for the taking. You are the beauty that is invested in the world.

The journey ahead will be a long one. Believe you own your power and in all that you are. You are no longer the warrior fighting for what you need. You deserve so much more. See yourself as a goddess and the energy that you extract from me will be just that. Goddess energy.

You are changing the dynamic of how you work. You are becoming the softer power that has more power. You no longer have to fight, so you need to step back and simply allow.

I have been there with you before. I have been your mother, I have been your sister and I have been your power but as a special and dynamic force that you will never experience on the Earth. We have never had a physical life because it was too containing for us. Ours is a spiritual unity and transition of the highest power. Previously, you have regurgitated information that has been shared and it's now time for your information to be truth and light and love. It's now time to own the world that you are in and to see the beauty for what it is.

You are the beautiful creation of God and light. You are the joyous child of fun; the true source of knowledge and power and you believe and need to have all that you have and are given around you.

Step into the world of power and the enlightening force that is surrounding you. The goddess within you is serving you and wanting you to grow. You need to stand in that space and see yourself with love and respect and own that space that you are in.

You are the love of the world. You are the peace that others seek. You are the joy that is given.

Allow your time to be yours and allow your time to be golden.

The silver that you wear is the reflection of purity, the sparkle that you have is a reflection of your soul. You sparkle and radiate the love that you are.

The masculine world is no longer yours to seek, the feminine power of love is what you have to offer and this will serve you well.

Blessings and light, my friend, you are the true source of beauty. Please stay that way.

Chapter 3

THE BIGGER PICTURE

From my years working as a psychic medium I have noticed how my beliefs and values have changed, along with my concept and understanding of the Spirit World.

I look back to my naive self when I started this spiritual journey over 20 years ago and how my ego-self thought I was connected to Spirit, who shared with me all I needed to know about the Afterlife. Yet, it was only through the wisdom that I have gained from reading after reading that I could see the bigger picture and it's beyond what I could ever imagine or grasp. When writing *Survival of the Soul,* I realized I had so much more to learn.

There are many teachers, authors and speakers that are 'experts' in their fields and many would say that I am one of those, but after having surrendered into this space with Spirit uniting with me for this book, I realize I have only just scratched the surface. At the same time, it truly amazes me what I have understood as a channel for the Masters.

Through the channeling with Spirit I see how the Afterlife works. What I understand it to be is much more complex than I have ever written about or previously understood.

Having channeled the recent messages and *felt* the energetic connection to the words, I now fully understand their messages and it is my job as their scribe to deliver them to you.

It is here that I must share with you how I identify the difference between Spirit (those who have passed over) and a soul (a living being). I choose these labels but they are the same thing: one is living life on Earth and the other has made its transition into the Afterlife.

We have so much to learn and having a connection to our own Spirit Guide will help open our mind beyond what we have limited ourselves to thinking. Many people ask me if I will connect with their Guides and guardian angels for them. My answer will always be the same: 'It's a personal journey and one that you have to do yourself. I can give you the tools to help you connect but that is it.' The reason for this is simple: you don't need me to do it for you.

We obsess over wanting to know the name and about the previous life of our Guide. These are labels that we, as humans, use to identify a spirit. But when I talk of Spirit, I am talking about the soul that was once a human. The human body is created by biology and therefore the body is 'given' to the soul. As we have understood in life, some do not resonate with the gender that the body has developed as and the soul doesn't feel like it fits. There are some earthly souls that do not identify with either gender, which is also the truth of the soul. When the transition of death happens we still hold onto the gender of the chosen identity for a while, and then it is during time in the Afterlife where this label fades, where the soul becomes genderless and is simply a soul.

When we connect to Spirit, it is our human mind and ego that need to know the identity of who is talking from beyond the world that we live in, and which is why Guides will give you names that identify as either male or female. This form of identification makes it easier for humans to comprehend the existence of Spirit and the connection that we have. So, if you ask me who your Guide is, I always reply that it's important for you to connect with them personally, especially as they have so much to help you with in life. And that if you want to know their name, give them a name. Trust me when I say they will soon tell you if they don't like it and will give you a name that is more suitable. This happened to me.

Guides change as our situations in life change. Master Guides are the only Guides that will not change. You chose them before you came to this world and it is their job to keep you on your chosen pathway. You have most likely already had a life with them in your many previous incarnations on this Earth, and they are often classed as soul mates. Soul mates are a fascinating topic and one I will cover later in the book through the channeled words of Spirit.

Trusting your Guide will give you a much easier life but it's our ego and stubbornness that go against what we know is right; this is the human way.

Previously, when I spoke about Guides and our team, I was given the word *hierarchy* from Spirit but there is no hierarchy. Why would we believe that one soul is more superior than another? It's the evolution of the soul that defines them. Some souls have lived more lives and experienced more situations and, as an earthly soul, have grasped the concept of a truly spiritual life and mastered the art of surrendering to the Divine. Others are still learning and it's these struggling earthly souls who are actually providing lessons about how to surrender to the Divine and follow Spirit.

Spirit is learning about the new age that we live in: the technology, the change in climate, the world's affairs... all of these are lessons that many Spirits didn't experience, so it's natural for them to be now learning through us as we journey through life in order to master the pathway for other souls as they come to the Earth Plane to help heal the world. And we all know the world needs healing.

It's in the cycle of life that we understand the dynamic of souls both here and in the Afterlife, and know the way that we help each other with our growth. It's quite amazing when we understand the complexity of Spirit and how we help each other.

United souls

The hierarchy of Spirit is much more complex than you can imagine. The truth is, there is no soul higher than another; equality ensures peace prevails in the thinking of the mind. Every soul has a purpose and each purpose may be different and therefore in the human mind 'greater' than another. But this is not the case.

Lasting knowledge that is obtained from your life on Earth gives you the source of the Divine. Each soul has a path and each soul contributes to the knowledgeable progressive way of the truth. The paths of those more challenged on Earth result in providing the lessons that Spirit needs to help make the path easier for newer souls coming into the Earth Plane and prepares them for the journey ahead.

It is the mind of the human that believes some are superior to others but it is not true; it is the evolving soul that shares knowledge that helps the new soul on Earth to grow. The evolution of the soul is forever changing and consistently growing. Souls unite to give greater knowledge.

The knowledge of a united soul is powerful and can be used in greater ways and with many souls that are transitioning to Earth.

There are souls that have completed their time on Earth and told to assist and help others. There are souls that need to grow and come back to the homeland in order to download and rest and then travel back to Earth to help others grow further. Yet their growth is not theirs to own - it's for the goodness of others. You may call them the teachers in life that challenge and help you on your spiritual journey.

These souls are the ones that will be directed by the source and be given knowledge for the masses to share. The Master is the voice of the Divine and the wisdom that needs to be shared. It is through this sharing that other living souls will grow and take the words of understanding to heart and live by the truth that they know.

However, others will challenge and fight for the ego. Whatever their purpose is, is the correct way for each individual, and it's the individual's right to see their way through the soul progression of the transition of life.

For many, lessons will be learned and wisdom will be clear. Yet you have life now, so live with your hearts open in that knowledge and believe that the truth will be shown to you when the time is right in the journey ahead. Your team will share this knowledge with you and the knowledge that will be provided along the way.

Share in the knowledge, beauty and grace and change your world in which you live; you have a purpose no matter what the lesson is.

We love you, friend. Trust in the love of Spirit.

Your Guides

Spirit Guides, teams of helpers, Divine helpers, Master Guides; these are all the same thing. We are the source of knowledge that you need to get through your life.

We are here to help you and you have to learn the lessons that are set in your life. We cannot simply give you the answers or there will be no lessons learned.

What's the use if you don't learn? It is a waste.

The ultimate growth is for you to see that you have learned the lesson and when the problem presents itself again, you will be able to maneuver through it beautifully and with ease and then you will see how far you have come.

We are here to present the obstacles in various ways, and it is through these lessons that you can understand the next step. Some are hard and some are easy and although we never profess to make life hard for you, it's through listening and the feeling that you will find the answers.

You are the only person preventing your way through life. It's your mind and the strength that you have in that space which many call stubborn and where you're not willing to see the lesson.

Life can be easy if you are guided by us and we will never let you down, but it's in the listening that you must learn. To avoid returning to the same habits as before, you must learn and surrender to the truth and the Divine Wisdom that is part of you all.

It's in the learning that you will realize that letting go of situations and circumstances, which may involve people, is key. Your mind, however, will restrict your thoughts and your feelings. You may know what to do but it's in that thought where you panic, and so you start the cycle of old habits again.

Understanding and having belief in the knowledge of Spirit and the team that surrounds you will help you. You have a team of chosen souls who you decided to take with you on the pathway, for the right reasons, and they will change and flow - for the divinity of your purpose. For the greater lesson that you have on the Earth Plane.

The lesson is sometimes simple and sometimes it is complicated - there are no two lessons that are the same because individuals are unique. It's in knowing that, that you can see the opportunity of change and challenge yourself. The growth will be greater than you can ever imagine and its sole purpose is for survival.

Trust and believe in the voice of the Divine and the voice of self; together they will open the pathway to the world beyond what you ever imagined.

Master Guides

M aster Guides are present within you all and you can connect to us and the source of knowledge, wisdom and inspiration that is given to you.

We are the source of that knowledge and hold the key that so many people seek.

Standing in your power and taking stock of what you have is encouraging to others as you progress on this journey, knowing that eventually you will pass on your knowledge to someone else and that you are changing the world, one conversation at a time.

Have belief and know that we will always guide you along. It's going to be an amazing journey for you.

Guides

There are many levels of Guides that you will work with over your time. You won't have only one, you will have many and we are here to help you connect and help open the lines of communication to the realms that you need.

Once you create a bond with your Master Guide, endless possibilities will open up for you and your life. We can help you with so many things in life if you allow us; you only have to say the word and we will step in.

The journey with your Master Guide will be intense but you will always remain in control. We cannot and will not force you into a situation or circumstance. We will, however, carefully and gently guide and coax you for your best interest and higher good.

We work with other forces that you will also become accustomed to. We all work hand in hand. Our energy is something that you will have to get used to. We are always around you so the energy that we share with you is something that you have always been used to, so even though we draw close to you, you will often not know we are there because you are so connected to us.

Our method of connection and the communication may be something else that you will struggle with, but over the course of time you will be able to understand and feel the differences in energy, the tone of our voices and you will understand how we can help you.

You chose us to act as your guide. We serve you and your best interests, so learn to trust us in turn. Open your heart, mind and soul and allow us to guide you on this magical journey.

Your journey will be powerful and incredible but only as incredible as you allow it to be. You are in control, no matter what, and we will support you along the way.

Your connection to your Spirit Guide is one of the most essential parts of your development. We will help fulfill your life contract. We will help you with situations that are tough and help you find the words to comfort others.

A brand-new dawn

Today is the brand-new dawn - an era that so many have been expecting for so long. You are therefore here today to witness the phenomenon that represents the Afterlife. A phenomenon that is commonplace to those gifted individuals among you.

A dream is coming alive in the hearts and minds of so many. A space is being born of love, comfort and hope. A place of sanctuary and a place to share and become one with others who are on a similar journey to you.

The world can be a tiring place and knowing that you have others to support and understand you along the way will help you and change your life. You will see this come alive within you.

The understanding and knowledge that you will observe through these doors will be something that will shine, and you will be witness to the open hearts of those who have created a haven for you in a place of love.

To us, our world is real; a place of everlasting beauty and peace, where darkness never touches and only light shines from beyond. A world where you will find love that is immeasurable and where infinite possibilities can become reality.

You have been guided to seek the truth and love and you will find them here in the messages that we share with you.

Your pathway will be lit with love and gratitude for you as you spread your wings to the openness of the world and share your light, changing those who come across your path. The ripple effect has started and you will follow it. Lead forth the way and as you seek, you will find truth.

Follow your heart and the love within you. We bless you on your pathway of life.

Self-investment

Your personal care is of importance. You owe it to yourself. Although we honor and embrace others that are on the journey with you, the time will come for you to step aside and look after the vessel that will carry your exceptional soul further and to lead the way.

You are only one person, one soul that will illuminate the pathway for others to follow. That pathway is sacred and solid.

You will need to learn about self-investment and understand that you cannot expect, you cannot want, you cannot need for this is your ego at work, and it will not serve you in the way that is right. It's time to let go of ego and allow yourself to be guided along and know that you will always be shown the way and that it will be clear and filled with grace and ease.

The journey that you must embark on involves goodness, kindness and love and you will share the love that flows within your heart when the moment is right. There will be moments that you are to help others through life, yet there will be also be a time for you to back away, never turning your back but just allowing others to find and establish who they really are. It's not your journey, it's the journey of the individual and the love that you show will help them on their pathway. Light your torch and show them the way, knowing that it's safe to step out of the light occasionally to process your own thoughts and evaluations.

Be well, my child, and know that we, as Spirit, will serve you well as you have proved your loyalty and love for us.

Your conscious wellbeing

Self involves internalization of that which is not conscious but it should be conscious thought that helps your wellbeing.

It's the belief in self that will lead you forward for others to follow you. It's the belief in self that you need when others are looking at you through a microscope.

It's interesting how people will judge others yet not look at themselves, so invest in yourself and know that it's your strength that will lead you through life.

Many pathways are dark but it's in that darkness that the truth is seen but often not acknowledged for fear of losing the self. But how will you know self if that is the case?

The light will shine as it has always shone. It's the light of the knowing, of what the journey on Earth is for you. You know the pathway as it was ingrained in your soul before life, yet it's for you to embrace and live. Others will judge but their judgement does not serve you. Rise above this and allow yourself to be love and beauty in accordance to your soul contract.

Knowing one's self is the truth that is needed but fear drives that force away. Fear of the destruction of what can be and what will be. However, it's within that destruction that new life will be made, new plans will surface and strength will be found. When all is lost, you will re-evaluate and change, and it's in that change that you will arrive again to where you are supposed to be. Investing in self. Investing in your growth.

Life isn't always sunshine and roses, but the challenges mold you to how you need to see life. When trust is broken it can be regained when you see the truth within yourself.

Many people are not seeing their light but when they see their self-worth they are able to lead the way forward.

Open the hearts of all and all will shine. Open the heart of one and that one will shine. Oh, such beauty will be present and then love will flow through all that are touched.

Believe in the self and know your worth, and invest in the knowing of you.

Let the light shine

Let the light shine above you. Ride the wind and the waves and know that your true path will find you.

You are truly deserving of everything. Everything you want and everything you desire.

Know in your heart that you will find the love for you and others and that you will not go it alone. We will walk with you every step of the way.

Only time will hold you back. You are working in the greatest way for your gift and your power.

We are so very proud of you and want you to know that we love you.

You are worthy and strong and you will show the world this with all that you have to offer.

There is so much for you right now. Believe and know it's true.

Don't waver or fall. Be strong and love it. You are going back to your roots and it's good for you.

Know that you can make a difference. Surrender to us.

There's always a shadow

Darker pathways of the night represent the shadows of self-reflection where you self-doubt and struggle with fear. Yet, the irrational thoughts of the internal mind struggle with the light. Where the light shines, darkness will be a shadow.

This is natural law, and the law that is moving throughout the world. It's in this ever-changing manifestation of life where you see the beauty, but you doubt the reality. It's time to stop.

There will always be a shadow but it's whether you allow it to cloud you or to just shelter you from the sun when you need a moment of clarity.

The sun may always shine but it's in that space that you will find doubt. And the respite that occurs when you are seeking, will come in the clouds, in the space and in the time that you give yourself. The truth will shine in the shadow but when you allow the shadow to cast its darkness over the soul, that is when it will be hard to maintain the truth and the light.

Seeking truth and forgiveness of self is the first step and is when you need to hold onto the light. The light that is shining will always be shining but it's the actual belief that the light is shining that will change your mind. It's through this mind-changing that you will see the Divine and the love that is given to you.

You are a child of God, truth and the Divine, and it's in that love you know that the light will shine on all. See it and feel it and believe in it.

When you allow the shadow to overtake your day, find the sun and stand in the light. Seek the love of the Divine and the truth of the source, for the light will always be present in the loving embrace of the word of the Divine.

We are always with you

We are always around you, so never fear and when you need us we will surrender to be with you.

Your surrendering to the light is something that is needed so that we can connect. Of course, you are going to physically miss us but we are here for you. Whether it's a special occasion or not, you only have to ask and we will find you in the beautiful land that you live in. Our love is immeasurable beyond words and we will always connect when you need us the most.

There are times in life that many of you celebrate but for us, we celebrate love and life that we have all the time.

When you whisper to us, we whisper back. When you sing until your heart is full, we are singing the words with you. When you dance until you're out of breath, we dance with you and fill your heart with joy.

We are always surrounding you with the love that you need. You may not always feel it and that is something that we cannot control; when a part of you that is not surrendering to the openness of the love of Spirit. But our love is there for you to see.

Look around you and you shall find the love that speaks to you in many ways. It's not conventional or fits in a box - it involves loving life in the way that it's supposed to be lived, which is without limitations or in a box.

Just look and you shall find us. The whisper in the breeze. The trickle of the water in the stream. The crispness of the snow as you step in to its freshness. The twinkle of the stars in the sky. The waves of the ocean that rush onto the shore. The bright lights that you see. The moon that guides you when the night is dark. We are around you always. Always guiding you, always shining light on your pathway so you can find your way.

For we are the love of the soul that you crave. We are the joy in your heart that you hold. We are the smell of the freshness of morning and we are in every life that you live.

Just look at the beauty that surrounds you and know that the love that you have is there for you to find. It's in your heart and your soul. You are the reason that we continue to be around; your love is mirrored in the love we have for you.

Hold your head up high and know that we are with you until the sun fades and it's your time to pass. During that passing, the light will shine so brightly and you will see us again. Our hearts shall melt, the souls shall collide and love will be unbearably overwhelming for we will honor your love always.

So, when times are hard and you can't bear to look at the sun, know that the sun is the warmth that we have in our souls for you, always.

We will walk the pathway of guidance with you and when you feel that you have nothing more to give, just search in your heart and you will find us, smiling on you, shining love your way so you can find you way back to the road again.

Always love with all your heart because that's how we love you.

Just be you

Staying connected to self is important. You must understand that everything is possible and that you are not contained. Your soul is not contained and is free to experience life and the lessons that it presents.

We will always work with you but realize that you are in control. You are not perfect so don't make life perfect – make it wholesome, make it truthful and make it about love. When you strive for perfection you will get disappointed. Perfection is contained within your ego, not the ego of others.

Those who judge you are not prepared to look in the mirror of change and challenge. Just be who you are and by living this way, with truth and love in your heart, you will see that everything is perfect around you.

Free your mind and your soul to the love that is created and open your eyes to the beauty that surrounds you. You are a child of wisdom and knowledge, so remember to serve with love.

We are here with you, always.

Chapter 4

CHALLENGES

Life is never easy. I have heard many Spirits say to me – that the earthly life is hell and the transition is just like falling asleep, no matter how tragic the incident, like waking up wrapped in the arms of love and going home.

I often wonder why we are here and what we are learning from this life. I remember my son Charlie saying to me, 'Mom, I wished I had been born in the 1950s when life was easy and there was no technology.' Bless him, but the reality is that no matter when you were born there are always going to be drama, challenges and difficulties. It's part of the path that we chose before we came to the Earth Plane, so that our soul could evolve and grow. It's then that we learn our lessons so that when we do transition, we can then help other souls who are next taking the journey to the Earth Plane.

When we as a society start to trust and listen to the power of Spirit and the Divine and be fully guided by them, we will unite together and start to move through the tragic circumstances that are causing our world so much pain and suffering. It's something that the Elders have mentioned many times in the messages that I have recorded and listened back to. It's quite amazing when we think about it and it makes perfect sense now that the message has been broken down.

When life's challenges happen, we can react and overreact and that is when drama happens. We have enough drama on television without adding the drama that we create in life. Give yourself some time and space when life throws a curve ball. Take a moment to breathe and use 10 minutes to re-center your energy. Even meditating can will bring us back to Spirit and to our soul. Take that time to open your mind and listen to the Divine guidance that is coming from within.

Grab a pen and paper and see what messages are coming to you. Then you can move through the issue that life has thrown at you.

Of course, it sounds easy but it does take practice. It's a discipline that is useful and helpful for getting through any situation. As you are writing out what has upset you, let the emotion come out on the page. It's in that writing that you will find the truth. Some would call it journaling, but for me, it's communication with self.

Communication on any level is crucial: we all need to have communication with self to talk it out and write without thought. Let all your thoughts, feelings and emotions out and then when you have calmed down, you will see the light. It's powerful and it's a way that Spirit communicates with us.

I'm a woman and we like to thrash out issues with our friends and get validation that we are right when something happens. But I have noticed that by using the above technique, I can keep my issues very much to myself and no one knows about them. I have a few friends that I share things with but, generally, I will have already used this technique a long time before I speak to them. That way I can have a more balanced conversation with them. It's not a reactive explosion of emotion, it's more of a well-rounded, insightful dialogue, which is much more productive.

Fear destroys any type of relationship and when you step out of love and into fear you are fighting a losing battle. By using this technique, you do the opposite; you step from fear into loving and honoring the self and seeing YOUR truth behind the incident.

Then you can decide on how you move forward.

Sometimes, you have to walk away from people and situations, which is hard, but it's also their journey. When you surrender to the pathway without control, you will find that these lessons get easier and easier.

Own your pathway in life and live life for you and no one else.

Life's challenges

Challenges in life are set and you are the one who has to live them and learn from them.

Never fear, for you are exactly where you need to be at this very moment. Only you can change the future and your fate. The past cannot be changed as it is there to learn from and from which to grow.

The hands of time do not stop spinning. They continue to turn and you continue to exist both here and in the Afterlife as one soul and as a togetherness that will unite the world that you know and we know. It's a place that is ever-lasting and a wholeness beyond what you can imagine.

Living your daily life is something that you desire in order to fill your heart but there are other ways to fill your heart and live your full potential; it's amazing when you know how to go about it. All you have to do is open your heart and to embrace the love that is flowing freely - the love that is within you. For you have the ability to love and you have the ability to grow and find peace and contentment within yourself.

Rise above those that hurt you and fly higher than you have ever flown before knowing that you have the wings to span a distance and can touch the hearts of many.

Breathe knowing that you are in the right place and the choices that you make and the answers that you have are the very ones that will lead you on to your potential growth and illuminate to you the valuable love that you have within you.

You are a wondrous being with a light that shines so brightly. You are the love that is seen in sunlight, you are the crispness in the air, you are the waves of the ocean, you are the universe and the universe is within you.

Allow yourself to blossom and grow and never fear because you are exactly where you need to be.

Life is one big lesson

The beauty of life is unfolding before your eyes. Know that you can survive within this space that you live in and call life.

Knowing that your life is one big lesson may be a comfort. The lessons that you live are lessons of growth and purpose and were chosen by you before you came to Earth. You chose your parents, your life, your loves and your challenges that you have to face. You came here with a sole purpose and that is to learn.

This learning is something that many people turn their heads away from wanting to find their own way, often struggling on the pathway, which takes them away from the real reasons they are here.

Knowing your purpose is something that is powerful but it's equally as powerful not to know and to be guided. Our guidance is paramount in your existence. Just believe in the powers that you have; your life, your love and your wealth.

Wealth is not something that you earn; it's the wealth of yourself. You are rich beyond your wildest dreams. You have your love, your life, your friends and family. You have all that you need. Your friends will be there for you when you need them, your family will be surrounding your essence when you desire and need them, and you have your love within your heart and soul. The very life that you breathe is a gift. Beyond that, who needs anything else?

For you are the purpose of the Earth, and this Earth is a learning place. 'What do we have to learn?' you ask. The lessons for finding peace within you and in your life. To find peace on Earth and to find compassion with man. Nothing more and nothing less. Knowing this, you can grow into the powerful being that you are capable of being and you can open hearts and minds, and allow the love to transcend into the universe so that you can heal and find comfort within all of life.

Blessings, my friend, for you are the journey that we seek and our words will powerfully reverberate through you.

We love you.

How you trust what you believe is Spirit

How do you trust what you believe is Spirit? It is very simple: You need to know that what your soul feels is real and then believe with all your heart that the truth is staring at you. It's the human mind and the thought that another will see you as wrong, which will lead to fear of rejection or fear of speech. But you have the Divine right to seek the source of what is right for you.

No one should ever force or change your opinion based upon what they believe, as this is a concept that is not what you call spiritual.

You need to have a belief of self and knowledge. So, when you have that moment when you need to believe self and to voice this, you will need to feel the side of you that understands it, within your soul, and speak from that place. It's a place that will always know your truth. It's just a matter of believing.

Opening your eyes to truth

Opening your eyes to the truth is very simple, my friend. It's about seeing balance and the other sides to people's lives When you are in the rigid ego mind that is the self-centered opinion of self, you do not wish to know when another individual is correct or has a more profound view than yours, so you naturally fight the idea or concept.

It's in this space that you cannot see or accept another's view. However, when you open your mind to possibilities far beyond your control, you will see that another opinion can be better than your own, and it's seeing that and accepting that which will help you see someone else's truth.

But there are times in life when you do not want to see another way, which is part of an individual's narrow-mindedness. If only you would allow yourself to stop determining what is right and wrong. When you are determined and in that mainframe, you are unable to explore another person's words. This is where you must view yourself as a reflection. If you are clashing, it's time to stop and walk away and find space to be equal again. When you are equal and are not challenging each other, then you will see clearly. This is about the preservation of self. Do not change your opinion to suit another, as this will not serve you, will o destroy your self-will and you will not know what is real for you.

Own your opinion but not in a stubborn and thoughtless way. At the same time, realize what your opinion is and what you know as fact. If the information is uncertain then you are unable to know the reality.

The conclusion that you draw about another person is one that you have to live with, so ensure that you are speaking from the truth within your soul and not from an opinion that will change your life forever.

There are many people in the world filled with rage, fear and anger. It is time that you see that this is unnecessary and adopt a position of exploration, find out what you need and seek what you know to be real. Again, the facts will lead you to the truth in which you believe.

Always be open to your mind changing as it's in that change that you will see many facets of what is being presented. Allow your soul to decide the truth.

The truth

Ah, the truth is a very interesting concept because it can change depending on the person. One person's truth is someone else's mistruth; therefore, it's not what is truth or what is right and wrong, it's about the believer of the concept. When you understand this, then you can move forward to spread YOUR truth, which isn't always the truth that someone already knows.

It's simple and it's about change. Changing opinions of those around you and changing your own opinions of self. You are allowed to change your mind because it's the free will that you have all been given. and what you feel fits right with your soul.

The soul knows what is right, not always what is wrong, for you and for self. It's in this space where you conform to a society's beliefs and structures. If your beliefs align with a particular society's, then you have similar view points. If another's differ to yours, then you have, in your humble human mind, an opinion of what is wrong. But what/ who is correct in this unjust world?

This is something for you to think about, as it's about the truth that lays within your soul and feels right. It's the connection of people who come forward and fit in a mold. This is why you find that collective mind forces come together in harmony to create for a purpose and why other souls collaborate.

It's a very straightforward concept and is called the law of attraction, as you have so named it in your world. It embodies and correctly states that you attract what you seek and that when you do seek, you will find. It's a simple law of the universe

So, what is truth? It's the feeling of what is right within your heart and your soul. It's liberating when you discover what your truth is.

Be the truth

The challenges that societies face are immeasurable. But it's the pressure to be seen and heard that people put on themselves that causes the dying age of society as a whole.

What happened to the simple life? A life that wasn't consumed by media and lights and where everything is made so big? This may feed the ego but what happened to the soul? The soul of understanding, compassion and love?

What happened to the caring world in which you lived where others unconditionally helped others out?

You live in a world of conditions and ego, of truth which is led by lies, a world of big but that is small. A world that needs so much you have forgotten the path. Let go of what you feel is real because it's the fake life that you believe in, fake smiles and fake warmth. Be real and live in the love and peace that is needed in the world for you to grow.

The growth is all that you need and the light in the eyes of the souls that are being born will lead the way into the future. It's time to live, to be real, let go of what's fake and be the truth that you want to be.

Believe in the dream and remember to be simple, for simple is real and real is the way.

Soul searching

The real life that you need to live comes to you as wisdom that is channeled through you by connecting to your soul. It is when you are connected to the soul, that you will understand the direction of that path of self. Self is the key to all you seek.

You see when you seek; you are seeking for self, yet you already know the truth inside your soul. It's been there for a long time and it is the human mind that has forgotten and neglected the hidden real truth. You hold a goldmine of knowledge and you will seek the truth of the soul, which will lead you to the real life that you need to live.

The searching could be endless unless you accept your soul's purpose in life. Nothing needs to be dramatic or challenging or big. You can lead a simple life of goodness and it's in this structure of the soul that you will see your purpose.

Your purpose may not be to change lives or to teach others, as this is not within your soul. You may need to learn and grow from the wisdom of others.

Your ego will tell you that your message needs to be shared, but if you find yourself on the journey of leading others to the source then it's what you need to be doing, without thought or reasoning or ego. When something is forced, the human mind is alive within itself and causes you to go through a cycle of greed, need and want.

Let the light shine and the Divine guide and you will go in the direction which is right for the soul. No one can choose as it's the choice that you made before you came to the plane that you call Earth. It's the difficult part of the human existence that you need to understand – that you chose the life that you created and you must live with that life. It's a life that you can change and it's a life where you can grow from.

You, as an adult, needs to know yourself and it's in this knowing of self where you can make the choices that will navigate you through the waters.

You can either flow or struggle, the choice is yours, but you decide how you move through life. Let go of the ego self and of the controlling mind and let your soul soar free on the winds of change.

Finding your purpose in life

Meditate and you'll find it within you. And you'll recognize your true purpose because you will feel it as your passion. You'll find it. You'll find it within you. You already have it there. It is captured in your heart. You know it.

Your journey is to capture the hearts of many. Your journey is to make people happy. Your journey is to bring a smile to people's faces. That smile will make them glow from the inside just by looking, just by seeing, just by touching.

That is your journey, my child, but you have to find that journey yourself as no one can find it for you.

I could tell you what it is but you may not believe me. That's okay. You choose your own pathway. You may go one way or another.

You will find your pathway. You will find happiness in your heart and you will see.

Everyone has a path to follow

It's the Divine right of each individual to come to Earth with a purpose. That purpose can be related to many reasons, some more complex than others. Many of those who have transitioned young are the teachers in life, and who are here to help others see the light. Some will lead you to the darkness and it's only then, if you see it, will you allow the light to shine.

You all have both sides, dark and light, which are simply the human sides of you. The lesson lies in understanding both of these and acting accordingly with love. There are some people that are here to continually learn and will not leave this life without gaining larger lessons, yet it's in those lessons that others can also learn. There are many that have led a life before and have been placed on this Earth for others to seek the truth of the voice that has seen the light. The light shines where the darkness has been and where they have risen above.

You may not know your purpose until the end of your life. You may think you know but it's not a plan that you can control, it's a journey of the known that is unknown to the human mind. It is only when the time to transition arrives that you can reflect on the purpose of your whole life. Everyone has a purpose in parts of their life and the roles that they play within others' lives. It's important to remember that and to see the light before you.

Choose wisely on the pathway of life and follow leaders that will lead you to the light and the source of knowledge that will help you to grow.

We are so very proud of you on this journey. Allow your soul to navigate the next step ahead of you.

Vulnerability

The ebb and flow of life is the enabler of the future, the teachers of tomorrow and the joys of yesterday. The wonders of life will continue to teach you lessons about the journey that you are on.

There will be mysteries and joys, there will be wonders and love; all of which you will encounter in this place on Earth. Embrace all that comes your way.

Opening the pathway to beyond is a challenge that many will seek and which will enable the discovery of self and soul.

You have the power to discover yourself. The journey won't end, it will continue and therefore you can discover new possibilities and ways forward that are right for you. There is no right and wrong, only love that will be shown to you by Spirit.

Spirit will only show you the way forward if you surrender to the Divine communication that it brings. With that, it will bring you truth, it will bring peace and it will bring love.

You seek answers and you shall find them on your way throughout life. The answers that Spirit enlightens you with will open your eyes, your heart and your life to opportunities that you didn't think were possible. They will light the way forward and show you the direction in which you may go. Alternatively,, you will be shown the opportunities that only you can take.

We cannot choose and we cannot control. All we can do is guide and show you the way. Your decision is your decision and the life that you lead is for yours in which to grow. But remember, you chose this path, you opened your mind to the world beyond and you stepped through into the living knowing what you had to face.

We will always help you but only for as long as you want that help and that representation of Spirit in your life.

You have the power to further explore this opportunity and to see beyond the mind into the soul of another. This is the truth of the soul.

You have to grow, honor and respect the journey that you are on, for it is ever-changing and everlasting on this journey through life.

Open your mind and explore the infinite possibilities beyond what you know.

Being vulnerable

To be vulnerable is a beautiful thing. Vulnerability is the raw truth of the soul that explodes from beneath the ego self of the human shadow. It's the parts of you that cannot be hidden behind and it's the side of you that needs to be explored for others to feel safe with your soul. The soul that merges with another, such as with friendships or lovers, cannot be true without the opening of soul and the cascade of real emotions that results.

It's miraculous to be in that place of vulnerability with another. It's the raw truth of what needs to be seen.

You all have vulnerability, yet it requires confidence to reveal it as it's a place that is often hurting and a wall is built around it with the ego and mind controlling it.

Practice being in that true raw self and realize that the only one that can hurt it is you. Others will try but it's the strength of your mind and the strength of the soul that will protect you. It's your right to believe in the words of another but when you sit in the place of soul, you will see the light.

If you choose for another to hurt you, then they will. But you can only hurt yourself by not exposing the truth of soul. Exposing the soul's truth is beautiful and something that you should be proud to do.

Find the soul, show the soul, believe in the soul and see the truth of the reality behind the mask of life.

Jealousy

Jealousy, hatred and evilness are all earthbound qualities. They are all here in this earthly existence. They don't exist in the Afterworld. Not there, no. This earthly space is sometimes toxic.

Hurt, bitterness, anger, deception; you will find none of these in the Afterworld. Nor will you find them with your soul family.

If you are true to your heart, you'll live without fear.

Chapter 5

COMMITMENT

Commitment in today's society can be a very scary word. It can do one of two things: it can send you into a happy place of security or it can freak you out, depending on what you are committing to in life.

I thought I was great at commitment; however, I realized that in my younger years it was something I continually escaped from. Never owning a house but renting and moving 13 times in 11 years, jumping from one job to the next before I found my calling – yes, you could say I had commitment issues. But one thing I realized is that when your soul tells you that something is wrong then it's... wrong. It's like the time I said yes to a marriage proposal thinking, 'Oh no,' and then not knowing how to retract it.

We all have those times when we feel we should move on to the next level or that we need to commit to something or someone. Whether it's a career, a relationship, a house, a lifestyle or even a diet or exercise regime, we cannot avoid it; however, it has to be right for you. No one else. It has to give you what you need in life or there is no use in taking it further. It's about knowing who you are and what you want and need. Your goals, dreams and aspirations are all things that you need to commit to but you also have to make sure that they are free-flowing and open to change.

Many people believe that once they commit there cannot be change, which is untrue – there *has* to be change in order to grow in life.

This is the one thing that I feared when I was younger – the need to change and have freedom – and I felt that committing to something would have held me back. I guess in many ways it would have done but I know that I could have achieved all that I have with or without it.

I have explored this subject and have come to understand that we have to surrender to being tied to something or someone, even if it's stability for a moment, and that this is what every human is striving for – a sense of belonging to something. Essentially, we are attracting like-minded individuals that are going to help us better ourselves or make us feel somewhat 'normal'.

But what is normal? The best definition of this is that we fit in and we are accepted. I guess that's why I feel 'normal' living where I do, Lily Dale, the world's largest center for Spiritualism, where people understand my life and what I do. I've become more acceptable. Even during my time on television, I found it a struggle to tell people what I do. 'I'm a writer,' was my usual answer as it didn't lead to a barrage of questions such as, 'Oh, who do you see around me?' 'What does my future hold?' 'Am I going to stay with my boyfriend?' Honestly, that was and still is the only downfall of my work, but I'm never going to escape it. It's human nature to be curious about life.

However, living here, I have found that when people ask me what I do now, I openly say, 'I'm a medium,' because it's accepted in and around this area. I have committed to the title but it's also freeing to be out in the open and not have to worry about judgement. I'm accepted.

I have committed more to who I am than I have anywhere else.

When we look at commitment we have to regard it on many levels, reasons and timescales. I believe timescales are the biggest concern to many because they expect commitment to happen within a certain time. Committing to something that has a restraint on it can create no movement or fluidity in life. People have *expectations*, which can cause them to become disappointed, especially when committing to another, a job or life – all of which can cause us to have restraints in how we are living life.

I am not one for restraint. If things need to change, they will. This doesn't mean I'm not committed, it just means that there could be a better way of doing things. It's about being open.

No matter what we are committing to or for how long, there has to be the opportunity to have freedom to grow. You can be in a committed relationship but still grow individually and have the freedom to explore your own dreams and goals. It's so important in life. Commitment shouldn't involve any form of restriction, as a human cannot live with restriction. The soul is free flowing, ever-moving, ever-changing and ever-growing. You are the soul in the vessel that you chose in life. Be committed to you!

To commit

Commitment is often a challenge to many as in this world of self-preservation, no one wants to fully surrender to the unknown. They find safety in what they know and therefore are willing to commit to this, believing it will keep them safe. But commitment should be to self. For the discovery of life. To the betterment of life and the evolution of soul.

Commitment can pose a restriction to some but be a safe haven for others, and so it's not for us to say what you should or shouldn't commit to. Whatever you decide to do, commit to yourself, as this will give you the freedom to grow, live and explore life whether it be as a single soul or a group of souls.

It is the personal journey of another that can sometimes lead you on a pathway that you do not want to be on. Facing that pathway and honoring that it is not right for you will gain the freedom to explore your own values and what they are worth. Freedom is the key, which is ironic because the word commit means to restrain and create a defined sense of entrapment in mankind. But this doesn't have to be the case. Open your mind to explore all that there is in the freedom of possibilities while still being committed to a cause.

Some may regard that a love affair could lead to a committed agreement of two that binds you together. This works for many, yet restrictions can be complicated and so there should be no boundaries but freedom to explore who you are as a soul without judgement. Love freely and openly without restriction.

This can provide a beautiful sanctuary when conducted in the right way - the way the soul needs to be open and vulnerable.

Believe that commitment can be good or bad. It's up to you how you decide to see it.

Stand in your power

Your pathway is yours but there is a new guiding light, which serves and helps people as they navigate and maneuver their way.

Some will fight you, others will let you lead believing that you know the bumps in the road as you travel on this journey through life.

Allowing yourself the chance to make mistakes will also enable you to grow and take the lessons that you have learned with you. Those lessons are there for you to help others and change lives as you start your work in changing and helping society's needs.

You live in a constantly evolving world and one that needs help and guidance. It's your chosen role to make that happen.

Just stand in your power, own who you are and believe in what you can do... It will serve you well.

Trust and belief

The power of trust and belief is something that everyone must learn in the world that you live in.

Never fear for we will guide you on this journey that you are on. You just have to listen and allow your mind to be settled knowing that we will give you all that you need to help you through your day.

The words that we speak will be clear but you have to listen and that is the hardest thing to do when you are so consumed with emotions, feelings and life. Life isn't simple anymore; it is consumed with work, necessity and greed.

The world is looking for endless opportunities for success and happiness, yet it can be found in front of you. A simple smile and a warm hello is all that is needed to brighten your day

The truth lies within you. We see that truth and bring that truth to you.

Take the words that we say and hear them as truth.

Take the words that are spoken in your heart as love.

Take the words that you sing as the beginning of your everything.

You are the soldier that continues to strive for a better day.

You are the one that we need to continue on this pathway of love.

Open your heart to the desires of your being and allow your soul to ignite the flame that is burning within you.

Be the light in the world that has become darkened with ego, be the brightness in someone's world.

Be the hope for a brighter future.

Be the air that others breathe.

You have the desire and the passion to now follow your dreams and to trust. Trust that all is well and it will be well.

Listen to us guide you and allow your ego to drop away and allow beauty to shine through you, as only you know how.

You have the trust, you have the faith, you are courageous and you are willing.

Believe and stand in your power and shine.

We love you, my friend.

You are a child of beauty

The pathway that you follow can be a long one but know that you are never alone. You may feel it but you will journey with other souls that resonate with the same vibration as you.

You are the higher vibrational level for the ones that wish to connect. Connecting to your soul and to your life is something that is powerful and that you are worthy of doing.

You are the one who is going to ripple out beyond to bring others on this journey.

Forgiveness will heal, love will rise and the passion will be discovered within the depths of the soul.

Your soul is immeasurable beyond what you know in your world. It's a place where we connect with you on many levels. You just need to understand the complexity and depth that you possess. You're a complex soul with the simple needs of love, spirituality, growth and purity.

You have the way forward and you just have to believe in all that you can do. We will always walk by your side, as long as you allow your strength to be supported by us. When the moment arrives when you do not know how you will face the day, we will bring forward the strength that you need and your soul will remain strong because you are strong and powerful, you will not break and you will connect.

You will connect to others who are like you, the positive being that you are. Of course, the darker forces remain but if you want to be present in that darkness, then darkness will surround you.

If you want to be light, then light will surround you. Stay in that place of warmth, love and connection and believe that you can live the life that you have been set to live in the Earth Plane.

Just allow the fire within to rage through you and find your passion and fill your heart with love... for you and others.

You are the one who is courageous so, honor that power within you.

Never fear, we walk with you always. Know that we love you always, for you are the child of love and forgiveness.

You are the child of hope and inspiration.

You are the child of beauty and peace and you are the child of you... Find you and connect to the grace that you are.

Be well, my friend, and believe!

You are a vital being

You are a vital being in this life because you are to carry your work forward into the world. To do this, you need to remain healthy and in a fit state of wellbeing. Your wellness is something that we are interested in but we cannot do it for you. All we can do is help and guide you on the pathway.

Lead by example and honor your work. Only you can do this. Think about it as a never-ending pit that you have to keep filling up. You have to fill your energy up. We have provided natural energy around you to utilize.

We are all creations of the Divine and the Divine source is energy- the energetic force that can help and serve you. It's within your reach, it's there for you to grasp, just take it and use it. We need you to.

It's beyond what you can imagine. It's there as your source to help fill your vessel with the life force that you need to keep you going. Honor what we are offering you and take it.

Re-energize at any moment you need to. Breathe, meditate and connect with the source of all knowledge that is provided along the way for you. Know that you are always given what you need and when you need it, so listen and don't fight it, simply allow the endless source to be with you.

Your own practice of meditation along with your breath–one is as sacred as the other. Just allow one to follow the other for it will serve you well.

Just know that we will always put you on the right track if you need it. When it's time to settle and relax, we will help you but you will find that it will not always be in the way that you anticipate or expect.

We will do what we can to keep you going for as long as your life path needs to reach completion.

Just listen to your mind, body and soul, and live your truth from your heart.

We want you to shine

You can have a beautiful way with words. We will show you how and if you allow us to guide you, you will change the lives of many.

We want you to shine in the way that we see you. Your beautiful light will travel through the hearts of many as long as you remain pure. We can't do that for you, we can only guide you.

We will walk in the pathway of darkness and show you the light.

We will open the door for you when it's closed. But you have to choose to walk through it.

Your light will always be shining, just know that we see it and we believe in you.

Love the way that you know how and never change your goal.

Believe in the power of your gift and honor it.

Surrender to us and we will guide you the way forward. Believe this with all your soul.

A pathway of guidance

Your understanding of people is essential in your important role. You have chosen to and set yourself upon the pathway of guidance, love and peace. You will share in the knowledge that is provided and we will guide you.

You will be shown the pathway but there are times when you will face challenges. You may not like them and may resist them because you do not regard them as opportunities for growth.

These challenges will open you to beyond what you can imagine if you surrender to the fact that they have to happen, whether it's now, tomorrow or the future. We will help you to grow because without your growth we cannot enable you to help others that need you. There are many that need the healing and it's your role and your mission to help them.

If you truly decide to step into this path and live your life journeying with us, you will need to see these opportunities as growth and nothing else. Remember who you are and what you can do. The signs are there for you to see.

Open your mind, your awareness and stand in your power and never forget who you are. You are a child of wisdom and knowledge, the powerful source of the creator and through whom the deliverance of messages will flow without the ego of others.

Stand strong, stand powerful and stand tall. Hold your head up high and remember we will guide you, so hold our hands as you surrender to the love and joys that a life with Spirit can bring and know that your lessons have already begun.

The light is within you

The beauty of the day is yours to have. You will only truly appreciate its beauty when it is taken from you. The smell of the air, the color of the trees, the hotness of the sun when it beats down on your back. You have beauty around you always and this is something that you must honor and appreciate.

The beauty is also within you and so allow the beauty to shine through. Your eyes are the windows to what we know as the soul, and your smile will radiate and penetrate through the darkest of souls so that they can see the light again.

You have the power to transform the lives of many. You will see the beauty in those who stand before you like the day that you are living today.

You are and will be touching the hearts of many before you. Never fear, for we are always around you when you are looking and seeking for the answers that you need. You only have to turn to us, the essence of Spirit that surrounds your being, for we are one with you.

You are the beauty, we are the beauty and together we create beauty. Just believe!

Soul growth

Every commitment will end in either a decision or a death. It's very simple, yet human nature complicates things due to holding on because they fear change. You are living a life in fear if you do not want to change.

Realize that there is a plan and it's the Divine plan of yourself, one that you have created that is committed to self-discovery. Honor that within your heart and believe that you need to change for your soul to grow.

The evolution of man is the growth in order for us in Spirit to learn. In this we see a new world and a bright new beginning that is approaching.

You are on a planet of change and it's in that change that you will prosper. This is for the evolution and creation of man, not for anything else. The Divine learns from the wisdom that you provide and you learn from the wisdom of the source. It's a straightforward yet unique in concept. It's a learning cycle that has never changed for centuries.

Open the awareness beyond your limited thoughts and see how vast the universe is. It's the knowledge and the power that you can gain from another that will lead you to new discoveries about life.

Always believe in the truth that you seek and the love in your heart.

Commitment to another

Can two individuals commit for life? Ahh, the golden question my dear. There are many that make it work but there are many that do not. It's the complexities of each other combined that can cause difficulties but if they have the soul strength to work this through then they will.

If two people are meant to be bound together through life then they will be, it's that simple. But complications in life will supersede the primary forces of togetherness and the free will of the communication will fail two individuals so therefore, if they choose that they are to be together, then they will be. Divine forces or not, they need to learn about what connects the human race - negotiation and communication. If they learn that lesson together then they will grow together.

When there is any fear in a relationship, that is when cracks will show. People who are meant to be together will be together, if not as lovers then as friends. You see, many people 'think' that they have to be with one person because that's the way it's supposed to be. And here lies the problem: they think it, they do not feel it and they do not live it. They go about life with the standards that have been set by another, yet that life is someone else's life and it's not their own. This is why there are many people who cannot get on well when married will remain friends, as it's their path to be together in one way or another.

You have to live by your standards and for what you want. Create your own formula for a happy and healthy life in the way that you know how. People's problems arise when there is too much emphasis on thinking and doing from past generations and they consequently lose who they are. You have to feel and do what is right for you.

Society is changing and it's in that change that new guidelines are set. You have to change to keep up. Principles remain the same, yet the change is flowing. So, remember to keep the core principles of goodness, respect, kindness and love and then everything else will flow.

This is the simple art of living.

Commitment and natural law

Natural law is something that cannot be changed but you will still find resistance to that notion. Forcing situations is going to be counteractive to what you want in life, as you are not letting life happen in the way that your plan has been set to.

The struggle of forcing others is not needed, as you are only forcing self into a corner and taking another with you. Mankind has created this pattern and it needs to stop. Stop the struggle and the battle and realize that all you can do is in your power. When collective minds come together, the strength of the united force will be overpowering and will take you on a journey of change.

It's incredible when you get to witness it from the place that we are in. The freedom that comes with opening your mind and creating a powerful force of nature is wonderful, exuberating and liberating. Yet only a few can do this without restrictions. Some of you need guidelines in order to keep boundaries set so that your journey stays true. This is very evident of today's society. This is about power and belief.

If something is meant to be, it will happen, no matter what. The pathway has been set, and although your free will could delay you some, you will always come back to the one significant moment when something has to happen because it's natural law. Remember the mindset that you create for it.

The negative will follow the negative and the positive will follow the positive. It's time to choose the pathway you will be on. When you commit, you are not changing natural law, especially if it's to be your chosen journey. But others can force situations. Again, it's the freedom that is created in order for that soul to grow.

The commitment to a pathway will be led by natural law only. A commitment for a period of time or a lifetime. This is what is right for the soul at the time and the lessons that it needs to learn.

Chapter 6

ENDINGS

I'm sure as you read some of these writings you are saying to yourself, 'Not everything in life is rosy and life can be tough.' Of course, and I agree with that. But what I have come to understand from my many years of working with Spirit and trying to grapple with the vast complexity of knowledge that they bring, is that life is simple. It's the human mind that complicates everything. If we just let situations go and find the strength from within, life does become easier.

We cannot control anything in life and that is one thing that we are all guilty of – control. We cannot control another's feelings or thoughts and we are certainly not allowed to get into the mind of another. It's as if there is an unwritten rule in the spiritual realm that we cannot invade another's privacy. But if we could, would we want to? It could be hurtful and damaging to us.

One thing is certain, that 'everything will be okay'. But it's in those times of not knowing, wanting to control and trying to find out information that we forget to be and let go.

My dear friend recently told me she's watched me just let things go over the years, and admired how easy I make it seem. I told her it is a constant struggle and that it's something I have to work on daily. I have a rule: 'No expectations. Just let life pan out as it's supposed to.' However, that doesn't mean I don't have dreams, goals and aspirations. That doesn't mean I am not let down sometimes because I have an expectation. But disappointment comes from our expectations, wants and desires. We cannot control things when there are other factors involved. Naturally, you can control your life – when you sleep, how you eat, the exercise that you do (or don't do) and your feelings – but when there are other people involved, you have to let go and be. There is a plan.

Following the guidance of Spirit and the Divine is something that hasn't always been easy but the more that you work with them, the more that they will help you see the pathway ahead of you.

Let me share with you a story of my own. I was told at the age of 32 I needed a hysterectomy. I was desperate to give my son a brother or a sister. My husband at the time was not bothered and always knew that he was not going to be a father of the biological kind. I was devastated. I started to look at having my eggs frozen and at surrogacy. It wasn't a new concept but it really wasn't something that was out in the open back then and the technology wasn't as advanced as it is now. Countless psychics had always told me that I was going to have a daughter and I longed for her.

You may be thinking that I shouldn't have put my trust in the psychics who had told me this, but I just *knew* in my soul that there was a girl coming.

When I was told that the hysterectomy needed to be done sooner rather than later, I wasn't prepared. I hadn't gathered the funds to freeze my eggs, I hadn't planned anything and my world was spiraling out of control. Not only was I having to cope with losing a part of me that gave life to another, I also was having to deal with decisions about a surgery I wasn't ready for. Life took a turn and I couldn't go ahead with freezing my eggs.

It took a long time before I could let all of it go. I had to accept that I wasn't going to have a sibling for Charlie and I wasn't going to have a girl to do girlie things with. I was just hoping that I would enjoy a granddaughter if and when that time came.

I enjoyed the next years going through life not really thinking about the time when I had to give up the option of having any more children.

It was almost 11 years later when I received a call that no one wants to get. It was my boyfriend who, without saying hello, said, 'She's dead'. I stopped in my tracks and words failed me. It was in that moment my life changed forever. His daughter's mother had died unexpectedly.

I looked at Charlie, who had just come home from school, and said, 'How do you feel about Katarina living with us?' He replied in his usual matter-of-fact way with, 'Well, we knew that was going to happen but we weren't expecting this... Sure.'

I rolled my eyes at him as if to say, 'Are you kidding me right now?' and to which he replied, 'I guess I have a sister!' It was in that moment the memories of previous years flashed before me. And suddenly here was my daughter. Certainly not in the way that I had been expecting but I was being given the opportunity to help someone to heal and to grow.

The first year was the most difficult, and boy, was it hard but I always knew that there would be a brighter side, always realized that there would be light at the end of the tunnel. Even on the darkest days when I wished my life would go back to how it was before, the light shone in a way that I never expected. It was a smile through her eyes that said, 'I'm sorry'. It was a hug that she needed from me to make the pain go away or it was when I was the friend after school that would listen to the drama of the boys who she happened to like.

The light started to shine brighter and brighter until one day, when Chris and I were sitting in the bedroom we looked at each other and smiled. The kids were laughing and actually communicating and that's when the bedroom door flung open and our three dogs (I had inherited one with Katarina) came running in, followed by the kids, and all fell on the bed.

'We want family time and if you are not coming out to us, we were coming to you,' they both said, as if rehearsed!

Without force, without control and without direction I allowed my life to go in the way that it was supposed to, and here I am with the daughter I longed for and the family I desired. It's quite amazing, really.

I'm not saying that the in-between years were easy, far from it. A divorce, several hard relationships and a major move all happened and there were days I wasn't sure I would get through the next minute let alone the next day, but I did. I came back to my breath and surrendered to Spirit. It was all I knew in that moment. I let go of fear and stepped into love.

Allowing life to take shape and by walking away from toxic situations in life is going to lead you to the life that you are supposed to be leading – one of love and harmony.

Truth and love

The truth and love from Spirit is all that you will know. It is the trust that you have within yourself. Your core.

This is your balance in all your life. The balance of who you are with everything.

You are at one with life when you see your true worth and value.

It's time to step into the journey of the unknown and believe that you will find the pathway of truth.

You will find the pathway of peace and the love in your heart will grow stronger than before.

Your truth is your truth and all that you will ever know.

You need to live by your truth and open your heart to the endless possibilities that life will provide with, and open your heart to the riches that you seek. Your riches are golden and within you.

Nothing more is needed but your integrity, truth and love. The rest will flow and the rest will be found.

Just believe in your heart, always.

Be well, my friend.

Helping others to see the truth

Complications arise when someone/something else, another human or interfering emotions, over-complicate a situation. This is when you need to focus on self because you are not responsible for another's emotions, thoughts and actions.

You must honor your journey for the Divine purpose that you have been placed on this Earth to fulfill.

This is all about love and when you come from the place of love, you will be given a purpose - one that helps and changes, whether you realize it or not.

Believe in all that you have and all that you are and stand strong in your beliefs in what is right for you and others.

Your spiritual gift

The journey that you are on is a long one, and it's a road that everyone has to take, but there are only a few in this world that will be able to change people's lives and make a difference, and you are one of them.

Embrace this gift in the only way that you know how. Fully embrace it and know that your Spirit Guide and helpers will stand forth and show that they are here and they will not let you down.

The journey starts with trust and trust is hard to find on the Earth Plane but you will find that the more you trust, the stronger you will become and your confidence will grow.

You have been chosen for this pathway for a reason. Know that the help you give people is going to be amazing and enlightening for you too.

Never give up and know that the changes in you will be reflective of the changes that need to happen on a conscious level all around you.

Stay strong. We are always with you and are so proud that you have taken this mission.

The Afterlife

With the ability to connect, you will shine through the darkest of days and you will provide the glimmer of hope that is needed by those who are in a state of grief.

Grief is a well-known place that many have been in and others fear. For us, it's a natural process and receiving souls who have crossed is a thing of beauty and love. We will take on the work that is protection for all. Your work, however, in your connection to the Afterlife is to ensure that the purity remains by helping souls who are on the Earth Plane to connect with souls who are here with us.

Allowing the love and light to shine through you is something that not everyone can do and that is something for you to be proud of and which is why you have been chosen for the journey that you are on.

Allow your love to shine in all that you do and allow the beauty to radiate through you in your way and touch the souls that come to you for peace and understanding. Show them that the love continues to grow past death.

Death is a stage that we embrace but you can make it acceptable in the lives of others still remaining.

Stand in the power of the love and know that the love will be shared with you and for all that you do for now and eternity.

You are a powerful being and a joyous soul.

Share the light of the word and the love of Spirit, for the love has touched you.

Be well, my friend.

The heavens are your home

Being in a space of peace and love is something of a joy but being in a place of love and peace within yourself is something that is a gift no one can take away from you.

The Earth is your home, the heavens are your home, and the love in your heart is your home.

Knowing that you are home wherever the place may be is true peace. Finding this is acceptance that it is available to you, but allowing this to be true is something that may take courage and strength. Your home is within the very essence of who you are.

You need to find the place and be.

Your growth will start from a tiny whisper that will lead to the fulfillment of what can be and that is peace. It's a place beyond what you know. Your love is truly worth valuing and acknowledging for who you are, and is the very reason why you are loved by so many. Your friends and your family gather to embrace you.

Do you know how many times you are shown love without realizing it?

Do you know how many times your name is spoken from someone else's lips?

Do you realize the value of your friendship to another?

You are the beginning of you.

You are the light that others search for.

You are the serenity that others crave. For you have the light of wisdom and the peace that radiates through you and that will signify that you really are home.

The end of the world

The end of the world is an interesting concept. There will always be an end but it is not something that you will see in your days or beyond.

The souls have to return to learn the lessons that present themselves. But there will be a time when the population will change and the Earth will no longer be the Earth that you know.

But this is not something that you will encounter, nor will your children's children, because the legacy is not ready to change just yet. There are many things that have to be dealt with before that happens, so enjoy the sweetness of the present and the connection that you have to all.

Finding your voice

It is simple: you open your mouth and allow the words to come out. You need to feel the emotions within you and find a way of bringing them out of the vessel that contains the soul.

You are the only one stopping yourself from speaking your truth and your mind. It's your ego and fear that will rule you, yet it should always be your soul and the knowledge that you have within.

This is the Divine knowledge of the source that you came with to Earth.

Believe and connect to self and you will finally find the truth that you need to live your life with.

Believe and trust in all that you have.

Gaining closure

Getting closure on a situation is something that only you can control. The knowledge that you have will lead the way, but it's the love that you have that will find acceptance to close the door.

The mind will complicate it all but really, it's very simple. You desire to hold on to the past, without letting go. Letting go is a simple fact of life because you are unable to control the thoughts of another or their ideas.

So, let go of expectations and find that you have love and accept that things are working out in Divine order to the way in which it has been planned.

How to help yourself

Your soul is ready to give you the knowledge that you need to help yourself. The heart has a primary notion of loving yet the soul needs to lead.

When others are able to connect with the soul then you can lead with the soul and the heart then follows. But for those who cannot connect with the soul, they must lead with the heart and find the connection to love. That is when they can let go of the sadness and find beauty in the end.

The love is what is going to keep you going. The raindrops that shower your day will help you see the bright sun that shines beyond the clouds.

Know that life is simple and yet it's made complicated because of what has been taught. This is a simple fact of peace and love.

Love will always be the concept that helps everything. Forgiveness and hope lead with love.

You need to open your mind to the new day of the morrow and help the love flow. Love is the only key that will help you through the transition that society calls death.

Endings

Endings pave the way for a new beginning. As humans state: 'As the door closes, another will open.' And although this is true, it isn't for all. The reason why it's not true for all is due to their viewpoints of life. When they do not want to see a door opening they will not see it. When they want to see an end, they cannot see beyond that darkness due to fear. It's a hard concept for some people to grasp and it's in that reflection that you can see the truth and the wisdom from Spirit.

We will always open a new door for you and for others. The Spirit World continues in that growth cycle even when you leave to transition. And so, the end becomes a new light of dawn.

For others that face the new day like a bright sun, they will find there will be dark clouds that come to pass. They do not stay yet they may linger for a time, and there will always be the sun shining on the other end of the spectrum.

Sadly, in a world like yours, the darkness has prevailed and there are not enough people who see the light. When everyone sees the light, the beauty of the day will shine in its glorious rays which will open the hearts of all to see and witness. But it hasn't happened yet.

You are in evolving times and it's a time of transition for mankind throughout the globe. This change will happen in 20 more years and you will find that there is going to be more lightness than darkness. There are going to be more smiles than sad faces. But it will not come without a price and so when you open your hearts to accept the truth, know that there is always going to be an ending that will be followed by a beginning and you will see the light of day.

It's as simple as the sun setting and the moon rising during the cycle of a day.

Be well, my friend, and live life for today!

Self-reflection and balance

The end is often the beginning and the dark is the beginning of the light.

Challenges are set before you return to the Earth Plane and the journey has been predetermined by no one but you. Yes, you have decided your journey and those that will impact your life during this time.

This is a cycle of life that is never-ending and will continue to evolve spiritually, emotionally and physically.

Surrender and let everything flow, for the journey will be easy when you let go. The control that you seek is something that is based in fear. It is created from the space of unwillingness to change, evolve and grow. This is a battle that is in your own mind but it's not a battle in your heart and soul, for the soul knows no boundaries and the soul continues to mold with each moment and situation that you find yourself in. Your soul is the ever-expanding knowledge of life that is yours for the taking. You just have to access that place and realize that every journey is possible and that every challenge can be overcome.

Holding on to the moment with a tight fist is only going to ensure that you lose what you have, because your mind is focused on not losing this space. But your soul knows that the moment has to change and that what you have now is a gift and what you have tomorrow is a gift waiting to be discovered.

Your goal, my friend, is to remain in the present and savor all that you have in your world. Your world of trials and tribulations are all there for your growth, and for you to discover the true soul that you are.

Your beauty is undeniably within us and shines for the world to see.

The beauty is the truth, the truth of the soul.

Chapter 7

GRATITUDE

We are unable to avoid the challenges that life presents and this is due to many reasons, but mainly they are there for our growth as a human.

You will understand from the following channeled pieces that our pathway is set for us in many ways but it's how you choose to ride through the storms that come your way is what you have control over. Some people find it easier than others. Our human mind doesn't have the capacity to process 'letting go' all the time. It can get tiring and it's something that you have to master the art of. I know because I certainly have to work at it daily.

When we look at what we have to face, fear immediately strikes and we become overwhelmed or consumed by the issue and then we understand that we have to let go of things that are not worthy. We have to ask ourselves whether it's really worth the heartache and upset the situation is putting us through?

We never want to let anyone down; however, we are all responsible for our own actions, thoughts and feelings. We cannot make anyone act, or have a feeling towards something, in a way that we want them to. Likewise, they are not able to manipulate us into doing the same. We all have to take responsibility for the part we play in any given situation or circumstance.

This has happened to me and one of the most valuable experiences in my life was working with a therapist who made me realize that I was only responsible for half of any issue. It helped me see situations in a different way and I never looked back. I started to realize that how I act in and react to situations is within my control and that I am responsible for my own thoughts, reactions and actions. How another person acts or reacts is up to them. So, if there are two people involved in a discussion, I am only responsible for half of any outcome. It helped me to understand any relationship where I have felt controlled, even where it was manipulative or toxic. I was 50 per cent responsible for my part, and that part was staying in that relationship and allowing the situation to get out of control. I am so grateful for this revelation.

When I saw it that way, I was floored. I never wanted to *own* any part of the situation because I saw myself as the victim. But in reality, I had allowed that to happen because I couldn't muster the strength or courage to speak up, voice my own thoughts and opinions because of fear. Fear took a grip and I couldn't beat it, so I was beaten. When I heard the words, 'Go back to the gutter where I found you,' come out of someone's mouth, I actually believed them and I found it hard to fight back. Instead, I cowered away with my head bowed low.

It was awful, but it was a huge lesson that I had to learn.

Slowly over time, I realized that *I* gave those words power because I *believed* them. I had to take ownership of them. And trust me, it wasn't easy to face the fact that, in my own way, I had created a situation that was toxic and had chosen to stay in it.

Hindsight is 20/20 as they say, and when I look back, I can see the reality but what is incredible was that I learned from those challenges. People who know me now would never believe that I was once the shy, timid person who wouldn't stand up to those around me and would allow manipulation from every direction.

Fear fed me. Yet it's through the hurt, pain and these experiences that I am now stronger than I have ever been. The growth is hard... Wow is it hard, but when you can look back on the life that was not what you had planned with situations you probably never thought you would have ever gotten through it, it's when this happens you realize how far you have come.

Speaking MY truth is paramount. But on the flipside, so is listening to it. If I am expected to be heard, I also need to listen. It's very simple, really. When you can understand that concept it's very easy to do. I am not responsible for anyone's emotions, so whatever I say, it's up to them how they react. Naturally, I'm not going to go out of my way to maliciously upset someone but if I have a feeling that is *my* truth, I am going to say it – in a nice way of course – but nevertheless I will say it. The younger version of myself would never have voiced it. I was the ultimate people pleaser.

To achieve this, you have to know yourself and be confident in who you are. When you realize that and know what you want out of life, then you can be confident about being that person. Complications arise when you don't know who you are or where you want to go, especially if you follow someone else.

Having structure and a spiritual practice helps. Yoga, exercise, meditation and any practice where you can stop negative dialogue churning around in your head are going to help. Your mind will become strong and you will find that with that, the strength will rise from within you and you will stand in your power. The soul can never be broken; the soul cannot be taken. It's yours and only yours.

Connecting with your soul is your compass through life. I suggest you sit with everything and *feel* how your body reacts. Your body is a reaction of the soul, meaning that your body will always react to what the soul is trying to convey to you. So next time you find yourself following the crowd and it not quite sitting right with you, stop and do what YOU know to be right, even if it's not what everyone else wants you to do. Be honest for your soul.

Surrender

Surrender and allow your mind to be clear to work through all that you need to work through.

We have presented you with people in your world who you need to have and be with, but you need to own yourself before you can reach the hearts that you need.

You are owning that space, slowly, and if you ask yourself clearly about what you need you will surrender to those that give to you and help you in many ways. Believe that you can do this and transformation is only a step away.

You need to open your heart to the love that you will find. The space that is held so tightly will release and surrender when you return home.

Opening the heart is truly a gift to you and others. There is no need for fear as truth should never be hidden.

It's time to step out and surrender to all that will be and all that is.

Manifest all that is golden

The oceans are set, the world is wide and the universe is vast. The limitations that you place on yourself with your body and mind are restrictions that you place on your life. The dreams that you have are the wondrous examples of the expanse that you can create but in reality, you place limitations on your world.

Let go and release. Surrender to what your world will be and allow the love to flow. For you have the power to create all that you want and choose to be in the world that you belong to.

The hearts that are shared and the smiles that are carried are blessings that we have in life.

You are the hope of the day, you are the brightness of tomorrow, and you are the joy of the future.

When you give unconditionally, you will receive unconditionally.

What you manifest will be all that you need. What you are given is all that you will receive. Opening up your world is all that you need for your dreams to come true. Step forth into the light and carry your ray of light with the love that you have in your heart.

Stand strong in the power knowing that when you smile you touch a soul, when you laugh you create joy and when you share you create love. For you are the bearer of the soul. For you are the knowledge of the universe and if you allow your heart to flow, you will allow others to do the same.

Manifest all that is golden. Manifest all that is simple.

You are the creator of your universe and you are the creator of your source.

You are the one that will touch others.

You are the one that will touch God. God is within us all and you can find the light within your soul that will radiate forward for the tomorrows that will come.

The simple pleasures of today will be all that you need to create all that you desire.

Blessings, my friend.

Allow yourself to shine

Be thankful for all that you have. Be thankful for all that you are. Never fear because your world is exactly how it's supposed to be. People forever chase their tails, going around and around in circles, and never see the light as they force a situation to be just so.

Life is to be lived and experienced greatly. Open your heart to the possibilities of tomorrow and leave yesterday behind.

Forcing situations will ensure that you remain in a negative cycle, so we are helping you to grow by allowing new opportunities into your world and closing the ones that no longer serve you. But people fight to stay in that space - a stagnant world without change.

The challenges that are in your life are yours and ones that you chose before you embarked on this journey called life. The situations that you find yourself in are the situations that you decided on to help you discover your soul and grow. It's the ever-evolving pattern that you and Spirit will eternally find yourselves in.

The cycle of change and evolution is the growth that is needed for you to appreciate who you are and for you to see that you can be strong. With every tear that is shed and every smile that is shared, your soul goes on a journey, allow yourself as a human, to connect with your own soul.

When you connect to your soul, you connect to us. You connect to the vibrational force, the Divine light that shines within you, that will brighten the darkest night.

You are a powerful force of energy and your soul needs to shine. Your ego and mind will try to stop this bright light from penetrating through into the world, but you have to allow it to shine and be the light you need to be. When you force your world to be how you want it to be, you are allowing the ego to take over the soul, and you, like the soul, gets locked away.

Allow people to see your light, allow people to see that space within your heart and allow it to be open.

Live with your heart open and free, allow your soul to be touched by us and allow us to show you the way.

You need to trust and open your mind to allow this new opportunity to take shape and to believe that you are worthy and respect who you are.

You are beauty, you are light, you are love in the world... allow yourself to shine.

Be well, my friend.

You have the power

The knowledge and power that you possess in your soul is remarkable. You hold the knowledge to the whole universe. You just need to believe that you can access it.

Connecting with self is the tool that you have to enable your guidance and understanding. You need to open your mind and explore beyond what you can ever imagine.

Your dreams are within the palm of your hand and your desires no longer have to be desires, they can be reality should you choose to step into the infinite wisdom and possibilities. These are all bigger than you can ever imagine and believing in limitations and confinements will only hinder you. Stand in the power and believe that. Open your mind and explore the side of you that you need.

No one can to tell you what to do. You need to follow your soul and feel the freedom that you have.

Let your mind be free and flow into the unimaginable and the unimaginable will become the imaginable. The imaginable will become the believable, the believable will become the possible and the possible will become the achievable. The achievable is within reach when you explore it.

Never let others dampen your emotions and dreams because you have the power to achieve. Your mind will try to taint your view but remain connected to self and you will achieve what your heart desires.

You have the power.

You have the knowledge.

You have the wisdom.

You have the belief.

You have you!

All you need to do is connect and believe.

The salvation within

The exuberance that you hold within you is the most powerful force that you will encounter within self.

You are a wondrous gift to the universe and the light that you shine is a ray in the light of the world.

You are the blessed warrior on the pathway we all encounter that is called life. You have the savior within you. You have the sacred knowledge that you need to get through the daily challenges of the world. These challenges are the lessons that you will encounter; they are the beginnings that you will seek and they are the oceans that you will cross to get to the other side of life. For you have the power and the knowledge that you need.

Never fear, my child, for you are the chosen one that will bring the messages from the source to the people. You are the one that will create the ripple effect. Even in your evolution of time you will transfer this knowledge and power to those who need it.

Your words are powerful, your words are safety and your words are all that people will need to hear the cry within themselves so that they can find salvation within. That salvation within is the peace that they need to face the truth and the love in any moment. That moment is all they need to focus on, each day.

As the moments flow into lengths of time, you will see the ease and the grace in which we exist. For you have been guided to give the knowledge that is needed to the world. Those moments are needed for others to heal, those visions that others will see to help them to believe, the voices that are heard will lead a pathway to us on the other side.

You just need to open your mind and expand beyond what you can ever imagine and know that you will find the truth within you.

You will never fail, you will only win.

You will never fall, you will only fly.

You will never die, you will only survive.

You have the peace. You have us on your side and now it's time for you to fly.

Enjoy, my friend, and know that we are with you when we hear you cry.

The wonders of the day

Opening your heart to the wonders of the day is always a joy each day and it's the opportunity of each tomorrow. Standing strong and believing in who you are and trusting that you have all you need to see the future that will manifest in front of you.

Stand in your power and be truthful to your life, your love and yourself.

You are the love that you seek.

You are the joy that you yearn for.

You are the hope that you need.

You are everything that you need. Just allow your light to shine through and believe and surrender to the moment of now.

That is all you need right now, nothing more or nothing less. It's time to own your life and who you are.

You are courageous and loving, kind and caring and you can see authenticity within you.

Never waver, for you will be guided on this pathway with hope and comfort, trust and love. Your journey will start with Spirit and end with Spirit. All you need to do is see what we see in you and trust, breathe and enjoy the journey with Spirit by your side.

You are truly loved, my friend.

It's all going to be fine

Oh, sweet one. Greatness and joy will come. Oh, how you are wanted and needed and desired for this work.

We are guiding and loving you through this journey of change and there is so much more to come for you.

You will change hearts and minds and souls and belong and grow and accept. Move along and you will.

Change is not far away. We have tested you and you are rising above so much. Just allow yourself to be free and know it's all going to be fine and that it's all going to be love.

Stand strong. The rest is yet to begin!

You are the one

The road you are following is never-ending so don't try to stop because you can't. You may take a twist and a turn in the road and you may also find that you are taking a diversion, but that diversion will always lead you back to the road that you are already on. It's called LIFE.

It's an amazing journey and one that should be embraced. Allow the challenges to mold you, allow the friends to change you, allow the circumstances to make you stronger for this is the way that life helps us to grow.

Be strong and realize that you are stronger than you think.

Realize that you are loved by many and know that your light within you will shine so brightly, it will touch the hearts of many.

Never stop believing, never stop receiving, and never stop giving.

You are the one.

Now, go forth on your journey and smile.

The beauty that you hold

Receiving all the love that you need for you to open your heart can be traumatic if you have been knocked down and then knocked down again after you get up. But you will be received by the love of Spirit and you will see the wonder that we can give to you for love of self. This is something that will not be replaced by another, it has to come from within.

You need to see the beauty that you hold. You need to see the love that you are and you need to feel the love that you have in your heart for yourself. When you can fully see that then others will also see the radiance that is glowing from inside of you. Believe in all that you are and the world will see this too.

Respect your being and others will respect it too. Love your own soul and others will love it too. Open this space of love for who you are and what you want and all the glorious gifts will manifest within you for you to live your life in the most harmonious way. Your life will open into the possibilities that you never thought were imaginable.

You are the power and you are the center of your own universe. Believe in all that you can achieve and you will achieve. The belief is within you. Just open your mind to the beauty.

Stand strong and keep the faith. We are forever watching, guiding and loving.

Be well, my friend.

A journey of love and understanding

The human mind is a powerful tool and can over-complicate the simplest of tasks.

Connect to the truth and the purity that is within you - the soul.

The soul is a powerful source of information; a communication tool for many to deliver the messages that we need to convey.

You are the one that needs to make the communication simple and easy to understand. The power that you possess within you and your growing knowledge will take you on a journey of love and understanding. This will also help others connect to the source of the knowledge that they have.

Being able to overcome the ego and the struggle that it creates will enable humankind to surrender to what is needed to allow these messages and our love to touch the souls of many. You are the one that will see the light within and know the universal love and power.

The love that is so pure that is there to be accessed by everyone who chooses to.

You have chosen the pathway others will follow for you will lead the way. Use the source that you have and the Masters will show you the way beyond what is known. Then through this you will search deep inside of you for the hidden truth and the golden knowledge that will enforce the lessons you have learned.

You are one with Spirit. Spirit is one with you.

You need to let go and surrender and allow others to follow your pathway and to shine your light. The world is your oyster. Just make it simple and use the tools you have around you. Have energy and love for all.

Be well, my friend, until the next time we meet.

Messages of healing and hope

The messages of Spirit are a valuable source of guidance for everyone on the Earth today. We will provide valuable lessons - joyous and momentous moments that can be shared across the globe. These messages are for healing and for understanding that what we provide is a life that is valuable and real and one that is eternal. The eternal life that is within us all.

The believers and non-believers, religious or not, need something to believe in and you are the one that will help bring forth the messages that are needed to help the world to heal.

The fighting that is within you all today is not something that you will witness here in the Afterworld. It is a world of love and comfort, peace and joy. We look upon your world with sorrow and upset but know that we can help provide the love and peace that is needed when the time comes for the transition for us all to become one again and for the evolution of man to continue to grow. And so we move forward, with you as our warrior of love.

You are the warrior that will stand upright, fighting to be heard and to be accepted with peace and with love in your heart, not forcing your words but sharing your reality. That is the reality that others will all come to realize when the time comes for them.

We will be waiting with arms open arms to embrace everyone, and with a soul full of love. Now starts a journey with us where we will touch the hearts of those who have been hurt, the souls who have fought and the bodies who have been wounded. We are there for all. No one is turned away and all are accepted into the loving space that we occupy and which is all around you.

The messages will change the way that others see themselves. They will stand with each other in a space of peace and love, knowing that the transition that they take will be one of love and healing. They will understand that pulling together will work better than pulling apart. When you accept the lessons that have been presented to you and work through them, this will help you in your journey of growth.

Without pain and suffering that the universe will not live in the way that it needs to. There will be no evolution and that is what you need... evolution.

Your world has not yet evolved to that space where there needs to be spirituality all around and so you are constantly learning and growing. But for those who are on that pathway, you will find peace, and love within you. You are the ones that we need to help the others to grow.

Your work is a battle of its own so fight it, you will win. Never give up. Know that you are the teacher that will share in the glory of the days of the sun, where you will help change the minds of the clouded and judged. You will open the hearts of many with your own stories of love. Show your true passion with each and every student you touch and know that you can begin your work, for now is the time to step fully into your power and embrace your world as it is today and change lives.

Openness, love and guidance for all will lead to healing and comfort through the messages that we convey. For you are the light of God, the God that shines within you.

Lead brightly, my friend.

You are perfect just the way you are

The power of your belief is something that is truly manifested within your soul, the enlightenment of self, and through the growth of soul. You have evolved to the point in which you need to right now. Nothing can be forced, nothing can be changed. Everything is exactly how it is supposed to be right now and all the change will come and go.

The ebb and flow of life and the relationship that you have with self are of upmost importance. Your relationship with others is only secondary to what you need. You are the growth that you need and you are the only one that matters right now.

If you are okay, then all around you will be perfect and fall into alignment.

The world is changing and the motion of the life that changes is something that some struggle with. But it's time to believe in what you want and what you desire in the world and it will manifest in the way that you need.

You are the believer of your own destiny.

You are the one that will journey throughout this time.

You are the reason why you are here and as for your soul's purpose... live it and believe in it.

All you need is who you are and what you become. Nothing more and nothing less.

You are the beauty in the world that you live in and you are the one that shines the light in your soul. Let it shine with love and grace and know that you are perfect just the way you are.

Be strong

As you connect with us, you will find that your senses are going to be heightened and will develop in a way that you never would have realized.

You will have some revelations and you will see some patterns in your life change. It's common for this to happen and if they haven't happened already, then allow them to and they soon will. Just be aware that they are coming.

Be strong.

Your learning is crucial. It helps us in the work that we do. You are helping to share the knowledge that we are providing and we couldn't do this without you.

Never failing, never fearing

The pathway that you take is yours and can be changed. You have the power to summon all that you need for your daily life should you need to make a change, but you need to believe.

Allow the times to change organically and with ease, never fighting or fearing, for this will only create angst and upset within the very core of your desires - your soul. You soul is a harmonious place for you to seek truth, not only about you but the others who chose to journey with you.

Some have come for the ride uninvited and others are lifting you to vibrations beyond what you know. It's time to shine and allow the journey to succeed in the way that you need.

You have the light that is within your heart, so you need to open yourself up to the world beyond. And to a life that challenges us for our own good, a life that shows us lessons when all we want is to dream, a life that will change when we want it to stay put. But it's a journey that is governed for you. And it's a time of growth for all concerned.

You have the beauty within your heart to shine like the bright beacon that you are.

Always allow the love in your heart to grow.

Be strong and true to yourself.

Never failing, never fearing... Your friend, Spirit.

Beautiful creature

The beauty that you have will radiate and shine through you in many ways and will touch the hearts and souls of many. You are loved and blessed with the grace of God within you.

Your journey through with mankind has been one of generosity, love and devotion but you have also been faced with the fears, the betrayal and the hatred; all of which govern how you see this life.

You are the beautiful creature that is surviving in this world of madness and knowing this, you can survive and hold a smile on your face and love in your heart - things that you are to be grateful for. However, there are many things to be grateful for. It's about honoring the self within you, the courage within your being and finding the strength to face each day when times are tough.

You are a gift to yourself and you are the present that needs to be opened daily. But at the same time, allow the heart to be opened by those who you may fear or those who may hurt you, and step into that space of vulnerability. You have the need to be loved and desired but you also wish to return it equally.

Your joy in your life is your responsibility, so allow your heart to be opened by the self-discovery that anything is possible and that you are being vulnerable to what is... And what is it? It's life.

A beautiful blessing walking this path on the Earth Plane, you are a gift to the world and you will discover what life can be. This is a true honor for those who cross your path and step into your life, whether it is for a second, a moment or a lifetime. For you are the savior to your own graces, you are the bandage to your own wound, you are the beat to your own heart and you are the song to your own dance.

Take that step into the beyond and know that you have the support and the love of the Divine Spirit and know that you will always be blessed. Never force or try to lead when there is nowhere to go, just allow the flow within you to find it's true path and that path will be enlightened with goodness and light. Never fear, just allow and be the brightness that you choose to be in the world.

Energy

O pen your eyes to the understanding and the concept of energy. Not everyone understands it and they don't see it in the way that we want them to see it. But once you start to realize the importance of it, you will know that we are only a moment away, just a thought, just a breath, just a whisper in the wind.

We are never far from you and we will continue to help you on your journey through your learning and ultimately in connecting with you soul.

Remember, we love you and are on the journey with you.

Chapter 8

HAPPINESS

We are all in pursuit of happiness, in one form or another. We release a concoction of chemicals into our body that give us that happy feeling that can come from various different situations and when we relieve the stress from our lives, it can heighten this emotion within our body. There is not anything that will come close to that feeling and so we are all searching for it.

There is an enormous amount of pressure that we place on ourselves, especially today, to achieve that we can lose the sense of happiness, even for a moment. We can't always walk around in life 'happy' but we can certainly be content.

I noticed it myself personally, only recently, when I had been striving to make something happen and I felt like I was juggling so many balls, I wasn't sure if I was going to drop them. Then suddenly my daughter said something to me and we both started to laugh, and it was in that moment I released the stress that had built up inside of me and I experienced an overwhelm of happy emotions running through my body. I felt lighter, my mind was clearer and I realized I needed to take a break. It had such an impact on me at the time that I thought about that moment for a while after. It was then that I knew I needed to find balance and allow a ball or two that I was juggling to fall and to pick it up once another project had finished.

Setting boundaries for myself is something I consider important so that I am able to focus and do what I need to do with balance.

Our false happiness comes when we allow something else to 'make' us happy. Maybe another person, a situation, shopping, food or a television show. These are moments that we allow another to be responsible for our emotion, yet it's important to find that emotion within ourselves. What I have discovered during my time working with Spirit, and through the courses that they have developed with me, is that stripping back to a simple life can lead to us to discovering what will provide us with true happiness.

When I was preparing my advanced mediumship courses, Spirit told me that I had to take everyone off social media for the duration of the online course. In a world where we rely on cutie puppies rolling around, cats knocking things off a counter and our favorite celebrity pictures to make us smile, I knew that it would be a hard task for students. We have the habitual routine of checking our phones to find everything, from where the item is in the food aisle at the grocery store to finding out what other movies actors have starred in. We are constantly turning to the Internet accessed by our computers and phones.

We want to keep in touch with our friends and quietly lurk and watch as your one friend is always drunk and you shake your head as if to say, 'Again!'

You watch others post pictures of their food as they 'check in' at the local eatery that they have visited for the fifth time in a month.

You see someone post old memories from four years ago of a time that they were running a marathon.

You watch how kids take a picture of a wall and write 'hru' over the image and send it to their friend.

You see the kids getting furious with one another as one of them has lost their 'streaks' on Snapchat that were over 45 days old.

I can hear my grandfather now saying, 'What is the world coming to?' and shaking his head in wonder before turning back to the paper which he used to get his news – not an electronic device that had a name and would tell you everything you wanted to know.

In a world like this, taking someone off social media, technology, novels, television, video and video games is a drastic measure but when Spirit told me to, I made it happen. By replacing all of those 'escapes' with meditation, communication, exercise, music and nature, suddenly my students started to see what was wrong in their lives and how they were not present with those around them.

They say that a habit takes at least 21 days to break and after three weeks of struggling with changing habits and withdrawing from any distractions, many of the students in my course said they felt calmer and focused but that most of all, they had discovered that they used these things to escape life which made them realize they were not happy and needed to do something about it. Many made life-altering decisions that opened the door to their true happiness and found that *they* were responsible for their own happiness and no longer relied on another person or thing to give them that instant concoction of happy emotions.

Happiness has to come from yourself – it is a connection to who you are and that feeling of contentment. If you are not happy then things need to change. You have to uncover what is going to make you smile and change your feelings, and you have to act upon it. It could be something small, like a new haircut and exercising or it could be life-altering, such a leaving a destructive relationship (platonic or romantic) and finding peace.

Whatever it is, you are responsible for yourself and for creating your own sense of happiness. No one else can do it for you. It's essential to find *you* and *do you*. Simple.

So, maybe write down a list of things that make you happy and ensure that you do one of these activities daily. This is self-care and loving yourself to help you find, balance, harmony and peace, all through the loving guidance of Spirit.

The concept of happiness

Ahh, the concept of happiness is the reality of truth. The truth of understanding what you need to survive in this world. When you understand this, you can then reach for the reality of what you seek. Seeking is one step but action is what is needed for you to achieve this sense of euphoria. A feeling of delight and joy, of happiness and love.

It's the love of self through which the happiness will rise, like when you do something that fills your soul, love will rise through you.

Happiness is the fire that will ignite within you. This fire cannot be lit by another; it can only be lit by yourself.

Happiness is the passion that drives you and when the force of the dynamic speed hits you, it is a moment that is overwhelmingly beautiful. The magic, the sparks, the love.

You are the truth and all that you need for happiness to be found within yourself.

Others mistake having a union to gain happiness, yet this is not something that is true. This emotion is temporary. It's the inner self of worth that will allow the happiness to rise.

Believe in yourself and all that you do and allow yourself to find the happiness within your soul.

The wealth of love

Accept the moment and live in the space that is pure and perfect for this time.

Perfection is endless but it is the beauty in the unseen that makes for perfection. Perfection is the flower that is starting to grow, it is the rain that falls that bringing life to the trees, it is the beauty of the smile from an innocent child.

The joy of acceptance is something that you embrace, for you have the innocence of the child and you have the joy of the day and the quiet of the night.

You have the love in your heart and a spring in your step.

You have the perfection around you, always.

The soul is hidden within but it's hiding in its glory of perfection within the space of self. Find the key and unlock the soul to unleash the perfect you, hiding inside your world. Imagine the possibilities that the exposed soul brings. Imagine the wealth of love that will be bought forward when you fully surrender to who you are.

Everything is perfect in your world - the choices, the actions and the situations. Everything is perfect for your life that you are living right now. Perfect for your lessons that you need to help you grow. You have the choices and you have the power. It's time to now believe that you are worthy of changing what you see to be not perfect,

Imperfection is not possible within a world that is as beautiful as yours. As long as everyone stays open to the exposed soul then the world will heal, the love will grow and the challenges will fade. We know this to be true. We have seen this but that will not happen right now. That space will happen in years to come, but know that it will be found within.

The moment in which you connect and embrace your soul, is the moment that you will start the dance of life, which needs to be danced to the full.

The experience of love will grow and you will be honored and embraced with perfection. Step out with your heart full and your love wide open to embrace the joy within you and your soul as you reach your perfect world.

Laughter

Laughter is the essence of all children and the essence of all souls. The joyous love that is shared through laughter is contagious and the future will be bright with this sound that resonates with the vibrations of love.

Smile and allow your mind to follow the smile and then the door for eternal happiness will open and the laughter will be shared throughout your whole being.

You need to discover your soul to be truly open - open to the laughter that is hiding within you. Never fear, for happiness and laughter surrounds you.

Your soul will grow, your vibration will rise and your spirit will soar to heights that encompass growth and that you have never seen before. You will rise above every challenge that is set for you with this vibrational essence within your heart.

Open your mind to what you have within your soul and allow laughter to be placed in your heart, mind and soul and touch others with this. Allow the sound of love to ripple through the world with you.

You are the one to start it and now it's time to open your heart and your arms and spread the love throughout.

You are one within us all.

Peace be with you, my friend.

Balance is the key to success and truth

Your idea of life is something that has grown with you from conception. It's been within your soul longer than the vessel that you carry on Earth. It's the contract that you have to complete your journey while you are on Earth.

These lessons are for learning yet there are also dreams and goals that you need to achieve and which will give you balance in life. Balance is crucial on the earthly life that you lead and will take you on a journey of peace and happiness. Without balance, you may never understand the other side to yourself.

The Earth has evolved into a saturated, polluted space of work and thought, technology and greed, want and desire, poor and destroyed lives. It's so sad that you do not see it as we do because you live it and are not able to see the full enormity of what has been created. The cycle that can engulf you and hold your life captive is toxic and it shadows your true self.

The joyous individual seeks fun, laughter and happiness. To discover this, there needs to be balance. Balance is the key to the success of truth and is a resource of life. No one succeeds alone in their work, they succeed with others that are like-minded and can pull together through achieving their goals and dreams.

Understanding the balance of mankind is what is needed for success. Some will show you the flaws and faults, the good the bad, the truth and the fear. This is the natural law of life.

You will gravitate to each other on this journey of success. Believe that you have these goals and you will find the truth to plough through the toughest times that create the strength of character that you need.

Be strong, my friend, and never give up on the dream.

The source of happiness

Happiness is within your own heart and soul. Others struggle with this concept of happiness, for it is seen by them as false. What is your happiness is not someone else's.

You need to open the soul and discover the beauty that lies before you. This isn't not a novel concept, it's something that has been within you all along. People struggle with being alone as this doesn't conform to the idealistic ways of what people believe to lead to being happy, but it's the individual's right to seek the happiness within themselves.

Reliability is now a pressure of the world. You find that you are reliable for another's wellness, but this needs to stop because it's false. It is not a fair statement of fact. Your level of contentment and understanding is what is found within you.

You are the creator of your own universe and are seeking your own missions and dreams. You can create all that you seek within the heart of your soul. This is the truth that you know and is the knowledge that you have. How can another judge whether this is right for you or what is going to change you? You have the responsibility of self to speak from the truth and share what makes you shine.

Search for your own soul answers that you crave to give you the understanding of life.

You have the ability to grow or not. You have the ability to lean towards the light as a flower would in summer, or you can shy in the shadows and not face the sun. It's the choice that everyone has.

You have the knowledge that comes from the source and understanding within your human mind to speak of truth and all of this is what we give to you unconditionally.

You are the source of your own happiness.

Seek and you shall find.

Peace

Peace. Your soul needs peace. Your soul is the place where you can retreat to when the world around you is out of control.

Sit and be. Find the peace within your soul. Be still.

You will find guidance and knowledge in this state of peace.

You have to make time for that peace and solitude to know that you are an equal to all of mankind. You are an equal to all who are around you. If you question that, then why? What is the point of questioning? It is a conscious lack of belief and it is the ego within self that draws out those insecurities festering within.

The truth is that you are equal, you are worthy and you are deserving of all.

When you come from the heart space, you will love those around you. You will love those who are in need of love and who are not finding the place of love. You will love yourself and you will love the Divine.

Love is always flowing through your heart but it can never be controlled through your mind. Love cannot flow in the way it needs when you are controlling where it goes and who it touches. Your soul is the space where you feel love, where you feel the truth and where you acknowledge the power within self. It's the driving force of the love that you have.

When we work together you are moving forward with the Divine; towards the balance of everything. Naturally, the ego will try to overpower in the world that you live but if you can recognize when that arises, you will be able to stop. Stop and breathe. Allowing the breath, which is the true life force that you have to guide you; it is the breath of Divine love, the source, and the power.

When taking all that you are and all that you will be back to the breath, you will find peace. You will find truth and you will find love. Let the mind stop and breathe and allow the guidance of the Divine to come from within.

Be peaceful in the world that you wish to live in. Don't get caught on the merry-go-round of control. Release and be. Peace is what you seek so go back to the space of soul and relax there in the comfort of wisdom that will be provided to you from the Divine.

Trust and be peace.

Chapter 9

KNOWLEDGE

Many walk this path of life not having a connection to anything but technology and a false sense of what the world is. Sadly, we are a changing society where people are looking down instead of forward. This has become a way of life for many due to loss, lack of feelings and/or searching for healing, truth and answers. Those who are on the journey of healing are searching but they won't find it, as the healing must come from within – within the soul space of self and some people find it hard to connect with.

I'm often asked, 'Where and how can I start my journey with Spirit?'

It's a personal journey and it's not one whereby I am able to 'tell' you what to do. It's a journey of flow and surrender. You go with the flow and you surrender to what you believe in.

This is an interesting concept for many because again, we come back to the concept of control. So, here's the cycle that I often witness.

During the transition of life and when a loved one passes over is such a hard time in someone's world and even the tiniest breath can sometimes be too hard. Over time, the moments of loss become easier to cope with but the emotions are endless and manifest as a constant stream of denial, guilt, relief, love, fear, anger, depression, sadness, contentment, upset, hurt and so on. We can find ourselves in that cycle and the search starts; searching for something that gives us some hope that there is an Afterlife, somewhere out there. Even the hardcore cynics start opening their minds to the possibility of life after death. It's called hope.

We start to look for a sign, we hear their name, we see a butterfly, a rainbow, a feather, a penny. 'What if it's a sign and I missed it? Give me another sign,' is the dialogue in your head, which is constantly and desperately searching, with the goal being the comfort that the loved one is watching over you.

Hearing a noise in the house and wondering who it is, who is sending you the penny, what does the rainbow mean? All of these signs have questions attached to them and again, it's our need to know and control. Thinking in the linear way in which we navigate the world.

But what if it's just Spirit?

Spirit as a universal collective force that is coming forward to help you overcome these obstacles? Would you be disappointed? Maybe, because it wouldn't be that one person that you were hoping for. But don't feel disappointed because this is a wonderful opportunity for you to step further into the progression of spirituality.

Imagine this: your loved one passes over and they are joined by their family and friends in the Afterlife, who are celebrating their arrival back home after the arduous task of life. 'Wow, that was some journey, dude, but you made it,' they say and love is outpouring from everyone who is with them.

Your loved one goes through their lessons and life review and then joins forces with knowledgeable and powerful souls who want to help others. Together, they are not individual, they are the collective and they are 'Spirit'.

One day you will be going through an issue in your human existence that needs some Divine help and you will recognize an energy coming around you. Yes, it's your loved one and you say their name, or tell them that you love and miss them. But then the energy changes. They haven't left you. They are with a team of other energies, ready to share knowledge and information that they want you to know.

Your human mind takes over and you again want to control the way the intelligence comes through and you start to ask questions. You want to take over without listening to the knowledge that they want to share. Emotions overtake and you miss your loved ones who are maybe connecting with you. This is only natural and the issue that you were initially questioning becomes something of the momentary past as you hear yourself saying, 'Spirit knew I needed them'.

Of course, they do. You have called for them unknowingly, so it's time that you stop, be still and *feel*. Be present and allow this moment to be the true gift of Spirit, to be the true gift of the Divine knowledge that is coming to show you the light and how to travel forward through this situation that you are going through. Take a moment just to be silent, to truly listen and to feel. You are being given the answers that you need. It's almost like a download of information that comes through you like a wave – a higher force of energy that is so light you can hardly notice it, except for the hairs that rise on your body and your sense of knowing that has heightened.

Be still when it happens and as it starts to fade, embrace the love of Spirit and your particular loved one who has cared so much to make the journey to match their energy with yours so that you will recognize it and so that they can give you some help. Thank them and the team that came with them to share their love. Bask in the glory that your prayers are being answered and that you are fully surrendering to the flow of Spirit and the Divine.

Believing that there is an Afterlife and then surrendering to the way forward are the first two steps when making the journey. Then you have to listen and feel and use the senses that you were given to unravel Spirit's messages.

You will often hear mediums say, 'Thank you, Spirit,' and that is because we have let go of who is communicating with us and we know it's the collective force of the Divine energy that is coming through us to help. The more you start to embrace them into your life, the more that Spirit will flow through you. You will have so many beautiful experiences with your loved ones, Spirit helpers and Guides, and the collective energy of the Afterlife. They truly are here to help you.

The two worlds

You are the voice of Spirit and without you, our world would not exist. We know that we can deliver the messages that are needed but the information may not be clear enough, so you are the messengers that the world of Spirit needs.

The knowledge that you hold is sacred and you can share that with the world that is around you. Know that we will be ever-present and walk the path with you. And know that you will be challenged along the way.

The path will not always be bright and it will have patches of darkness where you will feel alone but you will never be alone. This will test your faith, so allow the guidance to always be there for you. You just have to accept and know that there is so much that you can change and deliver for us.

The Afterlife is a life of happiness and a place where every soul can exist harmoniously as one. The existence is so tranquil with love. The sorrow that you know which takes you over will be replaced with only one thing - love.

This love is unconditional. This love is a place that is in your heart. Some of you love with your whole heart and some don't. That is okay because your love is right for you, but when you fully surrender to the love, you will embrace the world and the Afterlife as one. It's a place of everlasting beauty that can only be captured by living in the moment, in the here and now, and here as one of us.

Know that we extend that love, that beauty, that place of tranquility which is a dwelling that is vibrant and loving combined with knowledge. Hold this in your hearts knowing it is a place of being, just being you, the sharer of the love that we want to share in the world.

We love you and you are a blessing on this journey, for one and for all.

Creation of God

You are, my child, the creation of God. The higher being that we know serves and protects us all.

You have chosen well on this journey and so have we. We have chosen many to serve in the way that we need them to serve. Some have followed the pathway, others have deviated from it and haven't found the light back to Spirit communication.

Honoring Spirit through communication helps as we touch the souls of many on a daily basis. For our purpose is to teach and help others to grow. Your journey is to show others the way forward and to enlighten the souls that need you. You will change lives that need changing, you will heal the hearts of many and you will acknowledge that peace is needed in the world and that the world will change in the right way.

You are creating the wave that is needed for change. It won't happen overnight and the intent and the wish for it, is beyond what we can achieve. It will take several lifetimes for the change to happen. You will be starting the wave of new modern-day communicators that we so need. We need the purest of souls, those with hearts that are able to touch other hearts. Those with colorful lives that will teach the way of the light that we provide. The ancient source of knowledge is within us all. You are the one that will share this understanding and learning.

You will be the one that will open the door and allow the light to shine through. It will be easy and simple for you, you just need to believe. Your life will be given to you in a way that you have never seen before.

As this journey unfolds, the change that you see before you is the change that has to happen. You need to be prepared. The light will shine so brightly within you that it will hurt the eyes of many and they will shy away. Allow them to. Don't fight them. Just allow that change to be something that they need and you need. No control, just pure unconditional love that will radiate from you all at every given opportunity. It's your time to grow, to have the strength that you have never had before and for you to journey along with the others that are with you, knowing that you are safe and in the love of Spirit.

We will support you and provide you with a pathway of knowledge and love. Take care, my child. Your work is starting and your glow is within you. You are igniting the flame of passion.

Opening yourself up

Opening yourself up to the Spirit realm is probably one of the most rewarding jobs that you will ever have. There is so much that you can learn.

Your Guides will guide and teach you but you will also get much information from other people's Spirits, with whom you will communicate. You will never stop learning.

By opening up to the world of Spirit, you will gradually learn life's lessons in a way that you will understand, and you will be so much more aware of them than if you hadn't worked with us. Taking the time to develop your gift is not just something that you are going to do now, it's something that you are going to do either throughout your life or throughout the duration of your time working with Spirit.

You may come across roadblocks but these are just little setbacks. You will never lose the gift that you have been given. You may think that you have but it will always be there. And sometimes you will need to allow other things to clear out of your way before you will find that the gift is alive, underneath the surface.

We will always help you to find your way back to the pathway that you should be on. It may mean that you have to make major changes in your life but these changes are all part of the lessons that you need for you to learn to grow.

Rest assured that comfort in life can be gained from the knowledge that you will get from the world of Spirit.

We have come to help you in so many ways.

Allow us to help you. Do not resist and do not fight. Also allow us to help you help others. Listen, look and learn and you will share in the joy that the Spirit World can provide.

Be you, don't pretend, just open yourself to being guided. No ego, just pure unconditional love for everyone.

The key

M aster Guides are present within you all and you can connect to us and the source of the knowledge, wisdom and inspiration that is given to you.

We are the source of that knowledge. We hold the key that so many people have sought.

Standing in your power and taking stock of what you have is encouraging to others as you progress on this journey, knowing that eventually you will pass on your knowledge to someone else and you are changing the world, one conversation at a time.

Have belief and know that we will always guide you along. It's going to be an amazing journey for you.

The unknown

Challenges are set and some are overcome. And it's at that moment when you are unable to achieve clarity when you must step into the unknown – the unknown space – which will bring you peace.

Allow the space to give peace and allow peace to wash over you like calming waves. Delve into the waves of this feeling and know that the challenging path will open with the light of the way forward.

Trust and this will be true.

Seek the truth

The step forward into the truth is in your heart and what you know. You may not always see the pathway but it will be shown to you through the love that you have and when you listen.

Listen to the truth that you seek and find the answers within. You know the way. Find the courage to believe in your actions and not feel judged. The pathway is forward for you, which needs to be walked, yet when you are searching you will not find it.

When you follow and allow yourself to be guided is when you find truth. The seeking of truth will never cease. Turning to the guidance of Spirit will give you the power to look, yet have confidence to push through to the truth that you know.

Never fear, we are with you in the journey that you consider as the unknown. We are with you in a journey that we know is the truth.

Ask and you shall find, speak and it shall be given. You just need to receive and believe.

Chapter 10

LIFE

One thing that is apparent in life is that we have become a world of need, greed and want, which is understandable since we are a society that desires instant gratification and convenience. Children are being bought up with an electronic device in their hands and going outside to play in the woods seems to be a thing of the past. Of course, this is not a stereotype, it's a generalization. Nothing pleases me more when I hear kids playing outside and having fun, their laughter and squeals make me smile and fill my heart with joy. But sadly, we are teaching our new world to become insular and life is being lived through media. We are not living life in a complete way. Certainly not in the way that I remember.

As much as children are not experiencing the natural beauty that we have around us, we are also not investing in ourselves. Many are living a life where you work to survive and forget their dreams, and so life becomes a constant merry-go-round of survival. Just because you are breathing doesn't mean you are *alive*. Life is stressful and so we find that we do not have enough time in the day to focus on what we want. We escape the stress by burying our heads in television shows, social media, novels and shopping so as not to deal with the important things. Projects are put off and then we procrastinate. It's a cycle that some are finding hard to break; yet it's in the breaking of a habit that a new opportunity will arise. It's time to let go and find the space to do what we want and not what is expected of us, or what we should do.

We have to invest in our own self-care. It's in that self-care that we see what needs to change. When we allow ourselves space to just be, new ideas and thoughts and visions will come to us like a bolt of lightning. We will wonder, 'Why didn't I think of that before'?

So often we don't want to deal with our issues because they are difficult and we hope that the problem will go away. But it doesn't because it festers within our energy. True release is achieved by letting it go and giving it some air. Of course, it may be uncomfortable but once things are aired, then we can breathe. Our minds, which are often called our egos, are working overtime and when we step into our egos, we lose our authenticity. We must live from our hearts and souls, feeling what is right and wrong and allowing our intuition to grow and develop.

Our intuitive sides will flourish through silence. Be silent and the answers will be given. Some would say from Spirit, others will say that they are from God, or it could also be that higher self sharing knowledge that we were born with. Our knowledge rises from the subconscious to the conscious mind and is being given the freedom to swim around in our minds. It's in the silence that we are given the meaning of whatever question we have. Space is the key for getting the answers that we need.

Have you ever noticed that the word 'silent' has the same letters as the word, listen, and they are just placed differently? In silence, we listen, and we listen in silence. Perfect, really.

When receiving the wisdom of the Divine, you will want to share it because it is knowledge that you never expected to get – like a little bonus.

Never force a message that comes your way. Never try to tweak it to make it fit into your life or into the way that you want to hear it. Listen to it and don't analyze it. Just let it sit in your being and you will find the truth will surface without you realizing.

Take time to be in the presence of Spirit, to be in the beauty of nature and to love life in the way that it needs to be embraced.

Voice

Allowing yourself to have a voice is the gift that you give to yourself, for you are entitled to have flowing through you the words that Spirit speaks.

Never fear the communication that speaks through you, as the truth will unfold from the words that you share when you are connected to self.

Your connection to self is the key for all enlightenment and the journey that you seek. This is your time to stand up and be heard and to embrace the strength that you have within yourself.

Your mind expands to the consciousness that is within your capacity but the knowledge that is contained within you only needs to be given permission to be heard and you will then be that voice.

Stand up and speak from the heart and allow the words to give you courage as you open your heart to many on the same pathway as you.

Blessings, my friend.

The youth of today

The youth of today are the beauty of tomorrow and embody the learning and the growth that is needed for a brighter future.

The world is in need of nurturing and growth, and with the understanding of those that are following in the footsteps of Spirit and taking the lead, forces will collaborate and make a stand together if the right learning is provided.

Everyone needs to come together to appreciate the beauty that surrounds you and to allow that energy to glow. To dance in the moonlight and to share in the glory that is the universal force.

Believing that change can come and knowing that step by step each day and each bright new tomorrow, the world will be peaceful. Continuing the growth requires daily effort and should one person fall, the next will raise the energy to the level that is needed to ensure that we survive.

Everyone is the supporting evidence of the idea that by pulling together we can win, and that by pulling apart we create hardship.

The growth of self is there in order for you to understand the lessons that are now being passed down from those who have previously walked the pathway. It's a time of hope, comfort and forgiveness. It's time to open yourselves to the hearts of others, knowing that you are all challenging one another with the lesson and growth that is needed to thrust yourselves forward, thereby accelerating the growth.

The knowledge is before you and will become everlasting.

Open your heart and your eyes and your knowledge and know that your love will grow.

The compassion will be seen and the empathy will be felt. It's only a moment away as long as we work together.

The thoughts are collective, the moments are still, the sounds are creative and the beginning is the end of how we know things to be.

Seeing the bright future is the way forward to stepping into another's energy and to believe in all that we can provide.

We love you, friend, and be well.

The cycle of life

The beauty of nature around you is something that needs to be witnessed - the cycle of life, the ever-changing seasons and time that come before you.

You may be standing still and watching nature growing gently around you, yet you don't notice it all until one moment of the bright colorful array of nature is before you. This is the evolution of nature. Nature grows and changes while you are standing still. It's in that stillness that you will seek your peace and it's the moment when you will take time to hear the wind calling your name. You will notice that all you need to do is be still and in the moment because life will gently guide you along.

You will see the signs that will show you your next step and then you just simply need to act upon them. Spirit is alive within nature to help you. This love is there for you to experience and witness, always surrounding you and growing around you.

Just look and you will see.

Be still like the tree, allowing the wind to rustle your leaves and be a safe haven for all that nest within the strength of your branches. You are the tree, moving with the flow of life with strong arms that nurture those who come and rest upon you.

Be still and speak from your heart and soul and know that your truth lies within you. You will blossom and grow, you will move with the ebb and flow of life, you will open your arms to all that you love.

Be still, be present, be love.

The path is clear

The path is clear. Just look ahead and you will be guided. Know that life will take you where you need to go, on the magical journey for us all.

It's only a matter of time before you fully step into the power of all that it is. Structure, discipline and ownership are all you need.

Do not judge, just be.

You are here for a purpose. Enjoy this ride.

We love you.

Equality

The evolution of man is changing society and you need to be the leaders that will help others to see the light in the world.

Never fear, we are always behind you supporting you in the quest of change and you know that the change won't be easy.

See the process of change, think about it, and feel the way forward. It's easy when you take your mind away from your plans. You cannot plan something that isn't in your control. You are the facilitator of the change that is about to happen.

Peace will prevail. The world is changing and the way that the world is perceived is hard for many but it's truth and love that will change the way forward.

You know this truth within your heart, soul and mind. We are watching over you, showing and guiding you to the way forward but you need to be the one who takes action.

Many sit and wait but why are they letting life pass them by? They are not seeing the moment that they have. They are all hiding in the world and wanting the change but not being the change that they want to see.

You are all controlled in a world that is no longer free, yet you claim to be free spirits. Be that free spirit. Don't conform, instead allow yourself to be who you want to be.

It's about taking your life back and knowing that you can be who you need to be. Give yourself permission to do this and do not change, do not waver on this pathway of life.

Live life and don't sit behind the screen. Life is there for living and it's yours to take over. Be part of the world don't live on the edge of it. BE the edge of life.

You're a dream.

We love you.

Life is momentous

Life is momentous. You will never be able to get this moment back but this very moment, combined with many other moments, is what you consider life to be. Your life is your worth. The soul that you have and the life that you bring forward is what you share with the world.

Never fear, for we are always to you. The challenges that are set are only minor setbacks in the grand plan of the life that you will lead.

A life of fulfillment in every sense of the word.

You will lead the life that you have chosen in your plan and that life will morph and change with highs and lows and love and loss. But never fear for you will be guided along in this journey that we will help you with. You have desires that are so big, but do these desires serve you?

You have an opportunity to grow for you. Your pathway will shine with the life that you are wishing to live.

You are blessed and are on the road chosen for you. The road will lead to many others, so follow that life plan and enjoy this journey.

Open your heart to what you will experience through you in your life.

To be

Your challenge is not to do but to be. Be in the place of the Divine because all that surrounds you is well. Your journey is life and the challenges that are set before you are the ones that you chose. Your ego will force the way forward and will delay the process of joy, of happiness and of love

Momentary fulfillment creates a longing for more. Being in the moment is the truth, being steady with your way and not forcing your journey but to allowing it to unfold. The unfolding will inspire excitement and joy.

That moment is the truth. That moment is love. That moment is life.

The past cannot be recreated and the future has been written but not yet lived. Now, is the only moment that you have to live, so express that moment right now. Live that moment right now. Be in that moment right now.

Forever yours, my friend.

The addictive world

The changes that are going to occur are important for the evolution of mankind. We are stepping into a new generation containing souls that need the support on a level that you with your human mind cannot appreciate nor understand. This is where you can help with the guidance and love of Spirit.

It's a time of change and the addiction pattern is continuing, working from a whole new set of rules. The game is changing and it's going to be challenging to those who are leading the way forward. Those who are in the lead need to increase the awareness beyond what has already been given because the steps are about to change. So, they will need more in the way of guidance because these gentle and tender souls can't do it alone. You will witness more and more souls who need help but can't gain it due to fear. The fear will grow and then it will become more and more a world of addiction.

Awareness is the key at the beginning and at the end, with growth that is going to come from the soul. The soul has to be aware of the functions that happen during the process of addiction.

The transformation of the soul right now is of upmost importance. If we can get to them before this shift into addiction, it will help the recovery, bringing them to sobriety before it gets to the raw state. When that raw state hits, it's hard to transform.

I have faith that you can set this task in motion and that you will create a change that is needed for the generations to come. Addiction will be higher than ever, so it's a challenging time and one that needs to be monitored.

The addiction is not just about drugs and alcohol, it's addiction to everything. The age of technology has burnt a hole in the masses and is creating a generation of unhealthy beings. It is also creating destruction in the world – a cycle and a pattern that has to be changed. It's worrying and troubling and these generations of newcomers into the world have to discover a way of living without the constant need of being seen and heard, and then they need to appreciate the love that they have around them.

This needs to be addressed and it has been addressed, but we are concerned that the scale of the epidemic has grown beyond control. Using the steps to help each individual find the path forward is something that has to be done. They need to find the truth about why they are creating such an insular world for themselves. It is a world that is slowly dying through disease, destruction and hate, which need to be replaced by love and peace.

This is a fascinating but troubling time and the souls that are being prepared to enter the world are on a higher vibration to help this change. However, the generation that is in power and stand forth is the one that is damaging things at the surface of mankind.

People are conforming out of fear for reasons they don't understand because they are following the general consensus and then misleading the masses. People follow those few individuals who are leading the way and are challenging the views of others. Change is slowly happening.

You have to believe that change can happen and be prepared for it as it will be an arduous task and one that will be bright. Stay on the pathway of truth and love.

My purpose

This is a loaded topic. We have so much to accomplish and it's a challenge to help all souls, but it will be done. We are on a mission to survive and we are on a mission to regenerate society.

The world needs to be cleansed and it will be. Sacred places will need to be discovered and more land populated in other countries that will help the mission of survival for all. This is something that you will not see in your lifetime but in lifetimes for generations to come.

We are thankful that the life you lead is not the one that we led. No one is living a simple life and the stress of the world is now riding on the younger generations who witness a leadership that is failing them, which is why they are taking the personal responsibility for the growth of themselves. However, they do not realize this until they are in too deep and are then are challenged to stay present in this ever-moving, fast-paced society.

The world is now smaller than ever and the simple life has passed. It's time to grab the reins, take control, return to the simple life and trust in self, God and humanity. The soul is something that is alive even when emotions and feelings within are dead and when you cannot access that former feeling of happiness. You have all been in that lonely space where darkness surrounds you in a time of need and you do not recognize this until it's too late because the awareness in the world isn't there, and people associate this with failure. But it's not failure, it's growth

The technology of today is creating that driving force of addiction. Addiction is not healthy and it's something that is an epidemic of society. People are not understanding what it means to live. The generations of tomorrow will fear the outside world and not experience the outside nature of what the Earth provides. Earth will become a sad and lonely place with people searching for a false happiness that is addiction.

Chapter 11

LOVE

One of the lessons I have learned in this life is about love. Love for another, love for life and unconditional love. It hasn't been an easy lesson by far, but it's something that I have had to come to understand on my own personal journey and I'm sure that there will be more lessons to come. It has also become apparent to me throughout my daily readings, that having knowledge about different types of love on many levels has helped me help others. We all love differently and what someone feels is not always what another person one feels.

I remember someone saying to me, 'You don't love me how I love you'. And it was true; I didn't. For me, their love felt captive and not explorative and freeing, yet I was made to feel guilty for not loving in their way – what they called wholeheartedly. My emotions and concept of love was very different. To me, their love felt controlling but they saw it as being protective. To me, love meant being free and being open to explore. How ironic it was that we were in a committed relationship when we were experiencing polar-opposite feelings.

Love should never be a competition. There are always going to be different ways of expressing love and no two people will see it the same way. Love is so many things. It's security, freedom, and beauty. It is captivating, communication, fun… the list can go on and on. There are a variety of ways to express our love and I believe some of that stems from how we were raised as a child in this world. Some people express it in the same way as their caregivers did, while others express it in a completely opposite way. But what we do all do is learn through love.

Love was never freely expressed in the home that I grew up in, which doesn't mean that I wasn't loved, quite the contrary, but I didn't *feel* it. At that time, four people lived together in a house who were forced to 'love' (whatever that meant) each other. It was my naive understanding of love, which I struggled with. It was only during my own soul searching that I realized that we all did love each other but we didn't know how to *express* it. That was the difficult part. We never had the greatest communication skills and it has been only over the last 15 years that those skills have developed. And because of the love of Spirit and faith, I have finally developed them and now have a very open dialogue with everyone.

People express their love in many ways, yet it's often not received in the way that it's given. Gary Chapman opened my eyes when I read *The Five Love Languages*. I started to understand why my family felt so disconnected, no matter how close we were. Everything changed from that moment and I knew how others and myself received love and could consequently express to others that I loved them in a way that was important for them. Throughout my readings, I started to notice patterns that existed with other people. It was my very own patterns of miscommunication, misinterpretation, not knowing another person or how they expressed and received love.

Giving birth was the eye-opening experience about what uncon-ditional love truly is and I vowed then I would always show my baby my love. It hasn't always been easy, especially as I have been on the road so much and while he grew up we are like passing ships in the night, but I understand how he receives love and so I adapt my expression of it to suit him.

When Katarina joined us, I insisted on understanding her way of receiving love so that I could help her feel more at home and feel the love that we had in the family. Again, another life lesson for me about loving unconditionally and making sure that she felt loved.

Spirit has also taught me a valuable lesson in love and that is to create and live the life that you love. While life can be difficult and has its challenges, ultimately, life is a series of lessons and through those lessons we create a life. You have to find joy, happiness and peace and only you are responsible for that life. You are creating it the way that you want to, and through everything that you bring into it — the friends that you choose, the people you come into contact with, just about everyone in life, really.

When Spirit shows me a new teaching or course, they provide the exercises to help the developing intuitive or medium push themselves out of a comfort zone. The one thing that I have to do in my work is to love everyone. I hold no judgement, only acceptance of the person sitting in front of me or on the phone. However, there are times when I do find it hard to love everyone. Some personalities simply do not blend well, so Spirit gave me an exercise for finding something in everyone to love.

They taught me that I needed to see them as another living soul searching for a pathway throughout life and to open my heart to them: whether it is to how they style their hair, a sweater that they are wearing, their smile, or their laugh — just about anything to help me like them. Open my heart to love and accept them. This is a powerful tool and something that I have worked with for years. By doing this, you will see people differently and you can truly help them light the pathway ahead when they could be experiencing darkness.

Spirit and the Divine have given me the biggest lesson in love, and that is simply to love. Divine, God, Spirit or any other name that you decide fits for you is simply LOVE. It's the unconditional light that touches everyone without judgement. It's up to the individual to accept that love and be guided by it. Pure, unconditional love.

Believe in yourself

Believe in yourself and we will never let you down. Allow us to guide you and show you the light.

You will have choices to make and pathways to decide upon.

This is your journey and no one else's and we will be with you every step of the way.

Be thankful that you are opening your awareness in the purest of ways. You have an amazing opportunity to do this and to remain open. You have to continue to do this throughout this experience and know that you have the heart for Spirit to flow through you.

We love you and know that you will be guided in the direction that you need to take.

Connection and love

Aworld where we are fighting and hurting each other needs connection and love. That is what love is about, true soul love is about the connection - not just to another human being but also to self.

The realization of self is a powerful experience and one that should be cherished throughout your life and then beyond into eternity.

It is a love that is so vast that words cannot be used as there are no words for the infinite feeling of peace, completeness and wonder. It is a space that is filled with joy, that is overflowing and that you want everyone to know about. This is love.

Whether it has come from a lover, a child, a man or a woman, an animal or a friend, it doesn't matter, it will come. And you will feel that you have everything in this world going for you, even though your world may crumble in other areas.

You have to believe that you are worthy of the love in your own heart. This is the starting point to the love that needs to be shared with others. It's also a place of neglect because you don't want to focus on yourself or your own anger, resentment and heartache. But when you step back and focus on the pain that has happened, it manifests and grows in that space and is then multiplied again and again and is never released.

You will then bring that pain into the other relationships that will form in your life and you will share that grief, for it is grief, into the sacred space of love that has started to form. It's time to release those patterns and understand that you need to forgive and let go in order to grow and find the love, the true soul love and the purpose that you are here on this Earth Plane. Only you can find that place, only you can see the truth and only you can see the stars through the cloudy sky.

Open your heart and know that your love is waiting for you and it's time to release and feel free from this moment on. It's yours for the taking. Just step through and believe.

The gift of loving yourself

Light the spark that ignites the flame of true self, of the true passion for all that you have and all that you are. You are the only one in your universe that needs to matter in this moment. You are the one that will fulfill yourself daily and give yourself everything that you need.

Your love for self should shine through and this is all that is needed for you to embrace your true worth and love. This will then in turn bring the necessary people into your life, as they will be attracted to the qualities that you hold within.

You are the guiding force of nature beyond what you know.

You are the beauty that is in the world and you are the light that shines on the pathway.

Believe in all that you do and you will attract those who truly believe in themselves too. The likeness is the oneness that you share.

It's the ever-loving beauty of all. It's the ever-respectful glow of readiness to start the day with the brightness of tomorrow.

There is always the light that shines deep within you.

There is always the heart that is ready to love.

There is always the love that is ready to give.

This is all there within you. Just allow yourself to shine.

Understanding love

The understanding of love is so simple and beautiful and the human mind tends to over-complicate it.

The over-analytical mind throws everything out of balance and sends your world spinning into a cyclone of panic, confusion and emotion, dragging your heart down with it.

It is a necessity in life for you to feel the love from a fellow human, whether it be a parent, a child, a love or a friend. You desire and crave it, become consumed by it and you then forget what is important around you, which is you.

You are the vessel and the very essence that is needed to find that love that you so need. You are the one that others will fall in love with, but as you are constantly striving to find the perfect version of you, you then lose yourself. Spirit will set you back on the track and you are being prepared for your journey but you need to listen to your innermost thoughts and you will find us. We will guide you on your journey with clarity, wealth and wisdom – the essential traits that you need to navigate your world.

We will offer you the knowledge that you need but you need to listen and be prepared to see. We will place situations and people in your pathway so that you can learn the lessons and grow from them.

Life is only a challenge if you allow it to be. See it as a learning that you will grow from. Every person is a puzzle piece of you. You will have a wholesome impact on the world.

Every situation is the colorful picture that you are and every dark time will lead you through the tunnel where the light is brighter than in the last one.

You are what is needed in this world for a semblance of peace and that peace will ripple within others. You are the puzzle that will fit with others to create a picture of love - the love that is needed to bring peace to the world and for others to be inspired by you.

You are the inspiration.

You are the love.

And you will continue to raise the standard that has been set for the world.

Never stop believing in all that you are.

Never give up on your hopes and dreams and never stop loving wholeheartedly.

Memories

The lifetime of love is destined for all. Many believe the love of another is what is needed but love of self is of the utmost importance and is to be experienced.

The open heart is the true soul's reflection of all that is to come. The power that you have is in the soul, the love that you have is for self and the beauty that you see is for self. Everything else is a reflection of you.

You are the creator of the universe that you live in.

You are the master of your own existence.

You are the one that you shall love.

You are truth, you are one, you are knowledge and you are wisdom and power.

The doors of opportunity will open.

Within all of that comes love.

Let the love flow, my friend, and be the beauty within.

Love is free

Surrendering to your mind is something that you are accustomed to but surrendering to the soul is freedom. The need for control can overwhelm for the soul has a path. A path that is so free and enlightening that when you connect to us, it's beautiful.

The soul cannot be controlled as it desires only love, and love is free. Free to love, embrace and enjoy. There are many on the path of connecting that need to live more freely by opening their hearts to all that is around them.

Live the soul's purpose of love and happiness. Let go of tomorrows and live for the present. This moment is the glorious power that you have. Nothing else is certain except this moment and space - the air you breathe, the moment you're experiencing and the beauty that is ever-present in this world. It's a time and place we all need to see.

The world's beauty shines through you. Embrace all that you have right now. Nothing more. Nothing less. The time is now.

Allowing others to see that space within you to embrace others. The love that you have. The smile that shines. The joyous presence that you are.

Tomorrow is destiny, today is the present. Every moment will lead you to your destiny. Don't rush or the journey, which is magical and wonderful, will not be fully experienced. What is a journey without wonder?

Experience the journey as though tomorrow will never come. Experience life!

Be well, my friend.

You are the savior of tomorrow

Open your heart and be present in the love. You only have to step into the openness of the heart to feel the presence of love that is flowing. Everyone fights for love but no one fights to maintain love.

Busy lives create need and desires, but love is always present. This is a time in your existence when the world needs more love and appreciation. The time to love is now.

Allow your heart to be open and to find the love in all that you do. The ones who struggle in life or need the change, are the ones who most need the love, and so it is your job to bring the love back to them.

Open your heart and find the love within because all that seek, shall find.

You are the savior of tomorrow and it's time to open the strength within you and share it with all that need and all that crave.

Be well, my friend, and believe.

What the morning brings

In the stillness of the night
In the wonder of the morning of what tomorrow will bring
There's a space in my heart.
Will it bring peace?
Will it bring love?
Will it bring joy?

Opening eyes to the newness of the day
In the excitement and wonder
The moment in its glory
The joy that a tomorrow can bring.
Will it bring hope?
Will it bring salvation?
Will it bring happiness?

Opening your heart to the treasures of the day
Knowing that there will never be another moment like this
The love
The peace
The wonder that tomorrow brings.

The night

As I lie in the still of the night
Wondering if it's ever going to be right
The love in your heart that you know
That seems so distant and far away.

The journey you take daily
Guides you to different lights
Shows you different stories
Of people and what life can create.

And even though you move forward
Taking care of yourself
There's always the moment that shocks you
And you wonder how you'll pull through.

Just breathe, I hear
It'll soon be over
There's nothing that can be done.

The time that passes
The healing that's done
The changes that you make

Take you on a moving journey
Of magical moments and experiences.

So, as the single tear leaks from my eye
I look back upon life
I know the emotion that fulfills me
I know that love is real.

Shine your light

You have been chosen for the journey, and ahead of you, all is golden. You see the light where many do not. You seek the pathway of enlightenment yet the light is there. It just needs to shine.

Speaking your truth within your heart is like having the knowledge, yet some do not know what to do with that information that they have been given.

Own this moment in time. Follow the guidance that we give. We continually guide but we can never force. Some may listen to the guidance of others and ignore the truth of their own heart; this truth that is Spirit and the Divine source of knowledge that they need. It's the love that shines forth in that space that you have, to know is truth.

Some people seek and others will listen. Both are needed for balance and love. It is unconditional love that you have within your soul. People may wish to change you and turn you to their beliefs, but stand strong in your own belief and what is right for you.

You will always find those who are wanting to change you and pull you in a way that they believe is right for you. During these times, you need to sit and be.

Be with the guidance of the Divine and be with the voice of your true self. Never fear that your intention is misplaced when you are coming from Divine love. Not all can see when you are on your own pathway. Now know that you can do what you need to do.

No longer will you follow. Everyone has a different plan and purpose in life. When you are told what to do and you know it's wrong is the moment that you will do what feels right in your heart.

It's time to believe in the power of guidance from the Spirit. The true source of love is the Divine power that we call one.

Chapter 12

QUESTIONS: SOUL MATES, FAMILY AND THE AFTERLIFE

Having a connection to Spirit is quite remarkable but surrendering your vessel (body) as a trance medium over to Spirit unconditionally, leads to so much learning that simply flows through you. Trust and love make this happen.

In the beginning it took a while because I never fully wanted to surrender myself over to Spirit due to fear. I was concerned about not coming fully into my body, or that I would have 'bad' spirit energy 'attached' to me. I had all of these misconceptions in my head before I fully let go. I was inexperienced and somewhat naive as to how energy worked at that time.

I'd like to address negative energies. Of course, where there is light, there will always be dark – this is universal law. However, it's about whether we choose to give our power over to the negative side of things or not. If we do, we will only attract what we fear. So, for me, whenever I trance, I never worry that I am going to lose myself or that I will get a bad spirit because I believe only in the good and therefore I receive the good. Like attracts like – such a simple concept.

Another thing happens when you become a trance channel – you are given a wealth of knowledge that you can access and which is beyond what you will ever realize, even if you do not consciously remember what was said. It's like the healer who is simply the channel but also gets healed in the process. For me, it's as though I am not present in the room but my body is there. I don't remember the questions that are asked on a conscious level but after the fact, there remains a vast knowledge about the Spirit realms or life lessons that I just *know*. It's so interesting to experience it.

During my career, I was blessed to travel with three men: Ryan, David and Jib. They worked alongside me, helping to create the large audience shows around the world and watching me deliver messages was part of their daily life. We became like a family and bonded, which allowed me to unconditionally trust them to open myself as a trance channel.

I wanted to explore the concept of soul mates and one night in Norway, we decided that one of them would ask the questions that I needed the answers to and I would go into trance.

They piled into my hotel room and sat on the bed. I sat in a comfortable chair surrounded by very low lighting. I gave my usual talk about how my voice would change so that I could be led by the Spirits that would come through. I could tell they weren't prepared for what they were about to witness. I informed them to watch for visual changes in my body; that my hands may get bigger or my face may change. This was a new experience for them, especially as they had been accustomed to watching the glamorous medium who wears false eyelashes and 3-inch heels on stage.

The surrendering process was slow. I was nervous about their reactions and fear took over but eventually, I noticed my breathing became deeper and I felt myself slipping out of the back of my body and a force pushed past, gliding into the vessel I had left. A bit like how your foot slips into a comfortable pair of shoes. The following dialogue came through. I feel blessed that I retained a recording of the session.

Here you will experience Anu and Josiah providing answers to the questions about soul mates through myself as a trance channel. I had no knowledge of the information that was coming through until I heard the recording again. It was remarkable to hear it in the voices of Spirit.

Why is it that we may not meet our soul mates?

Why are so many people worried about soul mates? 'Why do we not our meet soul mate?' You do. You meet soul mates all the time. You meet them here. You meet them there. You meet them everywhere.

But people are so wanting this. They want this but they live in their heads, not in their hearts. They want so many things. Their soul mate is not the true soul mate, it is forced.

You meet them all the time. But the love you may not meet. That is why you ask questions. You may not meet the love that you want to meet.

You meet your soul mate in life but they may not come in the way you expect because you are all soul mates because you met before. Simple.

Can pets and animals be our soul mates?

Of course, they can. The soul is a soul. It's pure. It's a thing, just like I use this body as a thing. It's a vessel for channeling. It's a conduit for coming through.

Pets are so pure, which is why we love them unconditionally. The love they see is also pure.

Why is it that we are constantly searching for the perfect mate?

That is because you are human. You need to re-create. You need to have children. You need to procreate. That is the reason why.

You want to find the perfect mate who you spend the rest of your life with. But is that realistic? For some people, yes. For some people, no. It doesn't work like that in this life anymore.

In this life, we have to experience life. The spiritual being is about living. It is about living life the way it needs to be lived.

You have many lessons to learn and one person cannot make you. They cannot teach you all those lessons. You need to experience many things in life.

Those people who have loved many people, that's okay. Those people who say they have loved one person, it is not always real. For some yes, but not for all.

Love is in the heart, it's for the moment. And that moment will change - it will change all the time. All the time.

Be clear about who you love.

Do we always meet our soul mate?

Of course, you always meet your soul mate but do you love? You always love because love is true to your heart. Love is very true to your heart. It is about the experience that you have. The experience will come and the experience will go and then new experiences will come and new experiences will go and it is good. It will grow. It will grow so big and you will learn.

You will learn many lessons, many, many things, and many lessons for you will learn, from each other.

You have all met your soul mate. You have met others in your life and you are all soul mates. The reason is because you are soul-connected and you were meant to meet.

There is no mate, no one person. It's a soul. Why do people think it is just one?

Many soul mates will come and many soul mates will go.

Do we always end up with the right soul mate?

Good question. Your life is predestined. Your life is planned. You knew your life before you came here. You, my child, chose it. You chose the people that you meet and you chose everyone that will come and go.

You will always meet up with those you need to meet up with.

You will always grow with those you need to grow with.

You will always end up with those you will need to be with.

You will always love those you need to love.

How do we attract our soul mate?

We're talking about the one that you love, yes? You have to love from you. What is that? You have to love you. You have to love yourself. You have to find the love in you and love who you are. When you love who you are, you radiate that love outwards. It's a vibration among all the other vibrations that you put out into the universe and it will attract other vibrations. Therefore, you will attract the love that you need to attract at that time, and that person will step into your life at the right time.

You see, you are always, always on the right track and never on the wrong track. Many people make the mistake of thinking that they are on the wrong track but no, no, no, no. They are always on the right track, always on the right track for them because they have chosen their life. They have chosen the pathway of what they need to do. It is simple. Very simple.

When that person needs to come into their life, they will come. They don't need to go to a certain place. They don't need to be at a certain place at a certain time. They will be there when the time is right. Who knows when that time is right? But it will come.

Does love make us soul mates?

Does love make you soul mates? Not always, because you can love other people who do not serve you in life. But that is okay because they are there for a reason. It is so simple. You see, humans make it difficult. Humans make it so difficult. They push and push and push.

You can all love but you need to allow the love to come through. People are scared to love, so scared to love because of hurt, because of failure, because of fear. Once you get rid of those things it's simple. You just love, pure love.

If you strip everything away, love will still be love.

In the Afterlife, all we have is love.

When we are pure in soul, all we have is love.

What is the difference between soul mate and kindred spirit?

A kindred spirit is from the heart. A kindred spirit is one of beautiful love that you have to embrace.

The soul mate and mate are everybody. It can be a friend. It can be a lover. It can be a family member.

A kindred spirit is someone who is part of your soul. The spirit that is passion and drive. It's that yin and yang. It's someone who balances you.

Kindred spirits will show you the other side to yourself. They will show you sides that you will not like. They will show you many sides. You may not like that kindred spirit and you may fear them because they will really show you who you are. You may close up and you may push them away, which is normal.

Many people are looking for one person to love. But many people fear finding that person. They do not allow their heart to love like that. They do not allow their heart to love in that way because it can hurt if it goes wrong. It will only go wrong if the other person allows it to.

If two people who are meant to be together love willingly and openly, oh, it is wonderful. Sparks will fly. It will be beautiful. You will hear an orchestra play - amazing.

But there will be always something that will hold you back because of fear. Fear rules so many things.

Love freely. Really love freely.

That is the difference between soul mate and kindred spirit.

Is a soul mate forever?

The soul mate will always be forever. The soul mate will always come into your life. And then it may go, and then it may come again. The soul mate is someone who you are connected with within the soul family.

But you may be talking about soul mates for love. You will always have one love. You will always have one person that you will love and keep turning back to for that love. But that love will change. And that love may manifest in many ways, in many shapes, in many forms.

That love may be a child, may be a teacher, may be a lover. You may not love them in the affairs of the heart. And you may love them in many ways.

Does soul have a gender?

I have no gender. I am a soul. I am spirit but presently, I am occupying this body.

Technically I am female but when I was on the Earth Plane, I was male.

I have no soul. There is no soul, no sex, no age.

This is the direct transcript of Spirit when they were in my body.

What is a soul family?

et me explain. There are many souls. There are many char-
acteristics of souls. You are in groups, like families, and those
are your companions throughout life, the Afterlife, and lives
again and again. Those lives will continue and you will be connected to those souls again and again, inside and outside of
that life.

You will entwine all the time, like the branches of a tree. What will
happen is you will come and you will go after each of those lives.
Sometimes you will stay behind in the Afterlife. Sometimes you
will come back to help. Each time, you come in and out of your
soul family's life. The other soul families will do the same. That
is what happens. That is how soul families work. It is like you are
little groups.

There are four main soul families. They are like clans. They will
entwine and touch the souls of many. Many hearts, many souls,
many languages, many lands, many lifetimes, many journeys that
you will embark on, many lives that you will touch, many roads
that you will travel. You will not always be touching everybody in
your soul family, but you will all join up at one point in the evolved
universe of man. You will all have a journey.

You will all go back into the halls of the Akashic Records, which is where all of the families' records are held. That is an important place. You have to learn it is an important place where all the information about soul families is stored.

This is a very meaningful question. The clans then come forward. They are chosen. You are all entwined with each other, but you stay primarily within your clan.

You will see souls who will come and go. Souls will get taken from the Earth. Souls will get moved around due to natural disasters, and from other events that have to happen. Souls will get taken away.

It is not bad. It is what meant to happen. The soul family will help them. It is written in the halls of the Akashic Records. They hold all the information that is true.

Council of Elders has access to these records. The records are sacred and only a few chosen people are able to access them.

I have been one of them. I have been in the halls. I have sat with the almighty. I have sat on the Council with many of them. I have associated with the ascended Masters – the ascended Masters who are as one.

What a soul family is, is a big issue. It throws up deep questions and ones that will continue to be answered throughout time.

How do souls merge?

How souls merge is simple, my friend. The energy of another comes together in a fluid motion of love. This is why with some souls you see resistance and a lack of flow. This is because in this instance, two souls are of different planes.

These different planes are opposites, much like the opposite ends of magnets with the force pushing away rather than pulling together. This is the simple force of nature.

The world is very simple and it's the human mind with all its complexities that creates the inner confusion that you call life. So, by simplifying life, you simplify the natural law of life.

Let go of all that does not serve you and step into the truth of the soul. Let others into that raw space of realness within you.

Does family remain connected in future lifetimes?

Not always. Sometimes you are born into a family that you need to be born into because they will teach you a lesson. A lesson of growth - spiritual growth.

Sometimes you don't feel connected to your family and your family doesn't feel as though it's your family, but your friends and your fellows feel more like family. They are your family and your family can change through lifetime after lifetime after lifetime.

You have lived many lifetimes. We know you have all lived many lifetimes. You have fought many battles. You have, all of you, fought during many lifetimes together. We see and we know. We see that you have all been warriors and you have been brought together for one thing - to take the knowledge out into the universe to address a much bigger purpose.

I know we deviate from the question but you all have a bigger purpose here and in life. You must understand that purpose in life.

What if we choose the family we are with now?

Why do you choose the family that you are with? That is because you need to learn from them.

Many people will want to know the answer to this question. Many people will question, 'Why have I got this family when they hurt me so much?' But their family is here to help them. To help them grow. To help them learn. They are there for many reasons. They must remember that they have chosen their pathway. They have chosen their family and their parents.

You will grow and learn from your chosen family. You will journey on many walks of life with them.

Why do we choose the family members that we want to be with?

Because you feel that you can learn to grow from that person. You feel that through them you can learn many things from your heart. And that you can learn many things from your soul. They can touch your soul in many ways. You can see the beauty in them. You can see the purity in them. You can see so many things.

Because they are like windows that are so clean. So, you can see everything. That is why you choose them. You can see the pure soul. The pure soul is amazing.

But it's the life that they choose and follow that changes and taints everything and taints them. Then you think, 'Oh, I have chosen wrongly.' But you haven't, because they are there and they are helping you find your pathway.

How do we know what life contracts we have?

Your contract is about becoming one with yourself. This is the reason why I came in and Josiah left, because I know about the life contract. My name is Anu.

The Council of Elders avows that we all have a different thing to do. I deal with life contracts. I look at everyone's life contract and deal with them. I sit, I consult and I advise what people need to fulfill.

Everyone has a different reason for being on this Earth Plane. It is about being at one with yourself. You see, in this day and age, you as humans have now transcended into a totally different space.

You are now becoming more and more spiritually aware and spiritually open. The openness that you have is pure but you also need to let go of some of the things that are haunting you. You hold on to things that need to be cleared out.

Many of you call it baggage. It's a silly word but if you want to call it that, that's okay. That is your lesson, the baggage has molded you into who you are. It is beautiful. It's something that should be honored.

Your life contract was written before you came to the Earth. Everything that you have experienced is in your life contract. Your life contract is there for you to see.

You can access it through your dreams. You can access it through your meditations. You can access it in your quiet times. You can access it in many ways.

You can also access it through your own knowledge, by simply knowing. I am sure there were many times that you know things that you thought you were not supposed to know. That is your own knowing. That is your knowledge coming forward. You see, your own subconscious mind has been pre-programmed with all of the knowledge that you need to know in this world and in your life.

You are not supposed to know everything because then you wouldn't learn. What is the point of that? There's no fun in all of that, is there? You would just sit in your room - how boring.

We don't tell you everything. We want you to have fun and we want you to experience things. We want you to go out and see life. We want you to really see life.

And so, we don't show you everything in your life contract because it will change. There'll be these little twists and turns that will happen along the way. You won't expect these little twists and turns because you need to grow. And when these growth periods happen, you will blossom. You will blossom like the blossom on the tree.

Then you will change. Then you will become complacent again. Of course, that's when we have to say, 'Oh,' and give you another change. It's simple.

We can't show you everything in your life contract. I know many people would like to know everything in it but it's not going to happen.

Why do we call it the Afterlife on this plane if it's actually the place where we started?

I call it the Afterlife because it's a term that many people use. But it's actually a dimension. This is all part of the same universe. We are all part of the same universe and the Afterlife is just a dimension of this.

When you are in the earthly dimension, we are in this spirit dimension, and then there are others in another dimension. There are many different dimensions. It's very simple, but because you as humans consider death as bad or final and finished then you feel something has to come after that. That is why we call it the Afterlife.

The Masters say that everything rebirths and they talk about the new birth and the birthday. Often when a Spirit says that there is actually their birthday it means that they are being reborn, because they are being reborn into the other dimension.

Does religion have anything to do with the Afterlife?

There are many battles on the Earth Plane about religion but the Afterlife is straightforward. We all go back to the same place and where there is one God who is universal.

But God does not exist in the way that you would normally perceive. God is within you. He's what you see and perceive to be true. God is universal. It is the male and the female, and the yin and the yang. God is one energy.

Religion does not exist in the Afterlife. In this other dimension, there is no religion. We all go to the same place. The religion only exists in this Earth Plane.

Religion creates walls. It creates so many, many hostilities. It's something that really should cease but people need something to believe in. People need to feel something in their hearts. They need to have their faith. They need something and so we honor this, and we understand this.

It's a good question, but God is universal and God is with us.

What can we achieve in our lives through astral travel?

Another good question. You can see the universe. The universe is big. Astral travel is big.

You can explore many things. You can see many places. Many places are there to be explored in the universe.

To see, to explore and also, to learn. To learn and to gain knowledge. When you reach a higher self, you reach the knowledge you need to attain spiritual wisdom, and that is where we're working with you.

CONCLUSION

Hopefully, by now you have an understanding of how Spirit and the Divine work and an idea about the messages that they wish to deliver. Ultimately, these messages are about hope, love and growth. These messages also help you when learning your lessons so that you can flow more easily through life and learn to let go of situations and people that do not resonate with your energy. This is what I call the ever-changing flow of life – a concept that you can struggle with and not want to face when it starts to happen.

However, when you give your life over to the love of Spirit and trust them, you will be given so many blessings in return – so many opportunities and great people who are all part of the same voyage that you are on. It's remarkable how something that is not tangible is so giving.

We need to appreciate how much we are given in life through the love and the wisdom of Spirit.

So, in the Masters' words: be well, my friends. Until we meet again!

ACKNOWLEDGMENTS

Chris: Thank you for your endless support and dedication to a world that is so opposite to yours. You are a true gift and I am eternally grateful for the presence that you have in my life.

Charlie: You never cease to amaze me with your devotion and love, especially at those times when I have had to sacrifice our life together. I love you beyond words and I strive to be a better person daily because of you.

Kaylei (Katarina): Your world has changed so much yet I admire your strength and courage to 'make your mom proud'. Thank you for putting your trust and love in our creation of a family. I love you so much.

My staff: Thank you for your continued dedication to my work, for pushing me beyond my boundaries and for keeping me in check. You know it's certainly needed and appreciated, not just by me but by everyone. I couldn't do any of this without you!

Scott and Trudy: Your belief in Spirit, your belief in the work and your belief in people is inspiring. Thank you for believing in my gift and thank you for serving humanity. You are a blessing to this world.

Spirit: I can't believe you chose me as the messenger and I am truly honored and grateful to be given the opportunity to share your messages with those that need to hear them. You never fail to connect as long as I listen. I know you would love to slap me sometimes when I don't but then I wouldn't be human. Thank you for entrusting me with your knowledge!

INDEX OF MESSAGES FROM THE MASTERS

ABOUT THE AUTHOR

Lisa Williams is a world-renowned medium and clairvoyant with an amazing ability to communicate with those who have passed on to the other side.

Born in England, Lisa was discovered by Merv Griffin and introduced to audiences through two seasons of her own hit show, *Lisa Williams: Life Among the Dead*, along with *Voices from the Other Side* and *Lisa Williams Live*. All of these shows are now airing around the world. She has also appeared on *Keeping Up with The Kardashians*, *Anderson Cooper*, *Oprah*, *The Ricki Lake Show*, *Good Morning America*, *The Today Show*, *Larry King Live* and *Jimmy Kimmel Live*.

When she's not performing in front of large live audiences worldwide, Lisa offers workshops and courses in mediumship, developing psychic ability, intuition and meditation. In 2013 she launched the Lisa Williams International School of Spiritual Development (www.lwissd.com), through which she delivers her classes with her own unique and very hands-on method of teaching. Through the school, Lisa offers access to her personally trained and certified mediums and psychics who are part of the LWISSD Directory.

As well as workshops, Lisa offers a variety of online courses, from beginner to advanced levels. Her online video series, *The Confident Soul*, is aimed at building confidence within relationships and in the workplace. She is also the accomplished author of several books on mediumship and spirituality including: *Survival of the Soul* and *Life Among the Dead, I Speak to Dead People, Can You?* (retitled and republished in 2016 as *Was that a Sign from Heaven? How to Connect with the Afterlife*), and the insightful *Intuitive Soul Oracle Cards* designed to open our intuitive gifts and develop the psychic senses. Lisa is currently working on a comprehensive A-Z reference guide about the Afterlife and a book that explores the topic of soul mates and soul connections. You can find more details on Lisa's work and events on her website, www.lisawilliams.com.

Other products by Lisa Williams

INTUITIVE SOUL
ORACLE CARDS

44 Card Set and Guidebook

What if you were holding all the answers to the questions
about your life and were able to, through connection to your
own soul, access this valuable knowledge and make the right
decisions each day?

Well-known medium Lisa Williams and talented artist
Marie-Chantal Martineau specifically designed the *Intuitive Soul
Oracle Cards* to help you open up your intuition and develop
your psychic senses.

www.animaldreamingpublishing.com

Other products by Lisa Williams

WAS THAT A SIGN FROM HEAVEN?

This book is designed for those who wish to understand more about the Afterlife, to develop their natural gifts and to see the signs that indicate their loved ones in Spirit are with them.

By using this book, you will come to understand the history of mediumship, how to develop your gift, and how to notice and acknowledge signs sent from your passed-over loved ones.

You will be given daily exercises to enhance your gift and to help you connect to your loved ones and those of other people.

www.animaldreamingpublishing.com

Other products by Lisa Williams

DIVINE WISDOM AFFIRMATION CARDS

50 Affirmation Cards box set

Conveniently presented in a pocket-sized keepsake box
with a handy magnetized lid, the beautiful *Divine Wisdom Affirmation
Cards* offer 50 individual messages of love, hope and healing
channeled from the Masters by internationally celebrated psychic
medium, Lisa Williams.

To access the healing messages of the Masters, simply choose
a card whenever you're in need of guidance, or randomly select
one each morning to carry as a daily affirmation.

www.animaldreamingpublishing.com

Notes and Thoughts

Notes and Thoughts

Notes and Thoughts

Notes and Thoughts